Dear Annette, Mi

You both are amazing [unclear] time.
Love,
Lisa (Maia)

MW01594831

Missing Pieces

A JOURNEY OF DISCOVERY, FAITH, HEALING AND FINDING MY TRUTH

MAIA CHASIN

BALBOA.PRESS
A DIVISION OF HAY HOUSE

Balboa Press books may be ordered through booksellers or by contacting:

Balboa Press
A Division of Hay House
1663 Liberty Drive
Bloomington, IN 47403
www.balboapress.com
844-682-1282

Because of the dynamic nature of the Internet, any web addresses or links contained in this book may have changed since publication and may no longer be valid. The views expressed in this work are solely those of the author and do not necessarily reflect the views of the publisher, and the publisher hereby disclaims any responsibility for them.

The author of this book does not dispense medical advice or prescribe the use of any technique as a form of treatment for physical, emotional, or medical problems without the advice of a physician, either directly or indirectly. The intent of the author is only to offer information of a general nature to help you in your quest for emotional and spiritual well-being. In the event you use any of the information in this book for yourself, which is your constitutional right, the author and the publisher assume no responsibility for your actions.

Any people depicted in stock imagery provided by Getty Images are models, and such images are being used for illustrative purposes only.
Certain stock imagery © Getty Images.

Scripture texts in this work are taken from the New American Bible, revised edition © 2010, 1991, 1986, 1970 Confraternity of Christian Doctrine, Washington, D.C. and are used by permission of the copyright owner. All Rights Reserved. No part of the New American Bible may be reproduced in any form without permission in writing from the copyright owner.

Print information available on the last page.

ISBN: 979-8-7652-2534-9 (sc)
ISBN: 979-8-7652-2536-3 (hc)
ISBN: 979-8-7652-2535-6 (e)

Library of Congress Control Number: 2022918245

Balboa Press rev. date: 10/28/2022

Thank you to my husband, son, and all my family and friends who have stood by my side, especially on my tough days. Thank you for your genuine love and support.

My deepest gratitude to Tracy for being my listening ear and my editor-in-chief through this process. Our decades-long friendship has been an immense blessing in my life.

I want to dedicate this book to all those who battle mental illness (past, present and future). It is a real thing, and the fact that it often isn't visible makes the mountain of healing taller and harder to climb. You are not alone.

Pitter-patter, pitter-patter, pitter-pat, pat. One isolated raindrop causes no harm. As the storm builds, the drops accumulate; and before you know it, you're underwater, gasping for one breath at a time, frantically treading water, uncertain if the next breath will come.

CONTENTS

1

❖⟡❖

EARLY YEARS

I was wanted. My parents tried for nine years to have a baby. When I was born, I was adorned with love and attention and my younger brother was equally wanted and loved. We had an idyllic family and life, including a loving extended family, whom we saw often.

I started kindergarten, and from the beginning, I was a rule follower and wanted to please everyone. At the time, I didn't know what anxiety or depression were, but looking back, I recognized some characteristics of anxiety very early on. Certain events began to shape who I was to become and how I would perceive myself.

One wintry afternoon, the school bus stopped in front of my house after kindergarten. I stood up to get out and walked down the stairs. Unbeknownst to me, my coat had gotten caught in the door, and I fell. I was mortified and everyone laughed. You might be thinking, "No big deal." But I felt ashamed.

I internalized that shame. I felt that I had done something wrong, and that others were laughing at who I was. That memory and those feelings stuck. I don't know why I've always had difficulty letting things "roll off," but I have. This pattern became a part of my persona. Even at the young age of five, I began paving the stone path toward shame and self-loathing.

I was a kind child and liked to play with other kids. In second and third grade, several classmates decided to start picking on others who they thought were different. Hence, the commencement of the "they have cooties" game. I knew it wasn't right, and I didn't join in the teasing. The result was that I was soon a target. But amid the teasing, I continued to have a couple of friends with whom I did things after school.

My main memories of grade school were in fifth and sixth grade. I was targeted by a girl who emotionally and verbally bullied me. I didn't know how to handle it, and I started to believe that what she was saying was true. I felt alone and I cried a lot. I reached out to my parents, who were supportive. They tried to intervene, but to no avail. By sixth grade, it was unbearable, and I spent many nights crying myself to sleep. My parents, after many meetings with the principal and talks with me, decided that transferring me to another school was the best option.

Seventh grade was a fresh start, and I made friends quickly. I continued to be studious and a rule follower. I got involved in many activities and spent a lot of time with my family. Anxiety was not on my radar, but I tended to overthink and worry. There were things that in and of themselves weren't interfering, but when added together, they were signs of issues to come. Some of these signs were when I would beg my dad to get gas if the gas gauge in our car was at or below half a tank and asking my parents to double-check the house locks each night.

In high school, I was very outgoing and social, and I got good grades. I remember liking boys, but the feeling wasn't always mutual. I had my first boyfriend during my sophomore year, but it was platonic, which I realize now was a very good thing. Although I was fun-loving and things seemed great, I didn't have a lot of confidence. I was driven to be a good student and accomplish goals, and I enjoyed the affirmation and approval that came with those accomplishments.

During my senior year I was at a meeting for a club. We had to write down a nomination to represent our club as the sweetheart queen. When I was announced as the nominee, I was shocked. It hadn't occurred to me that I would be nominated, much less selected. Why hadn't I thought of that? Something inside myself had told me that I wasn't good enough, even with a supportive family and friends surrounding me.

2

✦◇✦

OFF TO COLLEGE

After graduating from high school, I went to college. I was interested in occupational therapy as a career, and I started on the path toward earning prerequisites to get into graduate school. I really liked my college experience. I was focused on my path, but I also had time for friends and fun. I began dating one of my best friends from high school. He came up to visit me one weekend, and things took off from there.

The interesting thing was that I never found him attractive. I craved attention and wanted to be loved, and he was the one giving me that attention and love. I didn't know who I was. Although it was a long-distance relationship, we were very close and saw each other when we could. We dated for over a year, until he broke it off. The breakup was upsetting for me, and I internalized that there was something wrong with me.

I eventually moved on, and I welcomed the attention I was beginning to get from boys. It helped me feel good about myself. I was in my next committed relationship during my junior year of college. In the beginning everything was great; I loved Kyle. However, after some time, he started talking about and introducing me to things that I didn't want and shouldn't have been exposed to.

Kyle shared that he had been exposed to pornography when he was very young by his older brother. It was clear that this was something that he was very into but being exposed to it made me feel degraded and horrible inside. I didn't realize the profound effect this had on my being, my soul, and how I perceived myself. This was extremely contrary to why God made me and my body.

I'm not sure why I stayed in this relationship that had elements that went against my beliefs and values. Our relationship continued, and after two years, it became long-distance when I went to graduate school. Something inside me was dying. Feelings of sadness were all too familiar. I went to the campus health clinic to address my sadness.

I saw a counselor once, but I didn't think it helped enough to go back. So, I went on with my daily life of studying and making the relationship work. There were many times when we were together that I would inexplicably cry. It got to a point that whenever we watched a movie with any remotely intimate scene, I would feel extremely uncomfortable and would break down, crying. Crying after being with Kyle and crying myself to sleep were becoming too commonplace.

Then, after three and a half years of dating, Kyle asked me out on a formal date. I knew what was coming. We were at a restaurant with a view that overlooked the city, and down on his knee he went. I faked the emotion and smiled, but I didn't feel happy in my heart. When Kyle asked me to marry him, I said yes. Why? That is a great question. I imagine it had a lot to do with my low self-esteem and with it being the next "step" in life, based on societal expectations.

The wedding planning began, and the date was set. My conscience kept interjecting that this wasn't right. We scheduled a venue, photographer, and florist, and we even bought the wedding dress and bridesmaid dresses. Even in the excitement of the planning, my heart sank. I was searching for a way out.

3

$\Leftrightarrow\!\!\!\diamond\!\!\!\Leftrightarrow$

THE WORLD WIDE WEB

I was in the throes of graduate school, growing ever closer to my graduation date and earning my master's degree in occupational therapy. During the period of my internships, I moved back home. It made sense to save money, and it was hard to find a short-term monthly lease. Now that Kyle had graduated, he was living and working two hours away. We saw each other on weekends, but things weren't any better.

I needed to feel connected and loved, and to find a way out. I wasn't actively or consciously searching, but I was searching. The Internet had been recently introduced and was now being used on a large scale. My parents had a computer on the upper level of their home, in a guest room. America Online (AOL) was becoming popular, and people from all over the world could connect electronically. Late at night, after my parents went to bed, it wasn't unusual for me to get on the computer and search the Web.

One night, I went into a chat room. I can't recall the topic that was being discussed, but I struck up a conversation with a man from another state. When he learned I was from Portland, he asked about fun things to do there and good places to eat. He was coming for his good friend's wedding that was a few months out. That was the start of my secret relationship with Drew. It started out platonic, and our nightly chats grew longer and longer.

It evolved into phone calls and, eventually, wanting to meet each other when he came in for the wedding. It felt wrong to be talking to Drew so frequently and feeling increasingly connected to him while I was still in my relationship with Kyle. At the same time, the way Drew made me feel was what I needed, so I overlooked any wrongdoing on my part. I was disconnected from Kyle, and yet, I didn't know how to—or have the strength to—break things off. We were far along in the wedding planning process. I was a shell of myself, but I put on a good face.

I then hesitantly decided to meet Drew when he came in for his friend's wedding. I was naive and trusting—too trusting. I remember driving to meet him in a restaurant parking lot. My heart fluttered with excitement and hope. By the time I met Drew, we had been talking daily for three months and we had a strong emotional connection. There was something about the anonymity, of not being face-to-face, which allowed me to divulge my truest self and be very open.

Drew drove up and spotted me. I saw him but kept looking around until he said my name, because he didn't fit his description. We got out of our cars, and as we stood talking, I realized something was off and I was not physically attracted to him. He looked old, much older than his twenty-eight-year-old claim. We decided to drive to a park separately and chat for a while. When we got to the park, I brought up the age issue. I was twenty-three. He quickly confessed that he was thirty-six. If I had been true to myself, I would have ended things then, but I hadn't found my truth, courage, and self-love at that stage of my life. I was disappointed that he had lied, but he explained it away and I let it go. We talked for a while, and after hugging, we got into our cars and left. He called me that night and I wasn't sure what to do. He wasn't what I had expected, but he made me feel so good about myself. He came and went for the wedding and our online and phone conversations continued.

I was brought up Catholic, went to church, and believed in God. I'm not sure why my actions over the next few years didn't follow suit, but I easily justified my actions. I got over the age difference between us, and Drew and I continued to get closer. I overlooked the fact that he was going through a divorce and that it wasn't finalized. He had conveniently held back that information until we had a strong connection. He sold the story of his wife being horrible, and I bought it. I had questions along the way, but he explained everything away and I was beyond wrapped up in our relationship.

The next thing I knew, Drew was flying into Portland as he was connecting to other cities for his business trips. We saw each other often and I fell hard. I was completely in love with him. He treated me like a princess. I felt like I was the center of his world and that we needed each other.

4

✥◈✥

DECISION TIME

By January my heart was stirring, and I knew I needed to make a decision about my relationship with Kyle. I knew it wasn't right to marry him. We weren't right for each other, and I didn't love him. A few weeks prior, I had invited him to go to a concert with me and my parents to hear the singer for our upcoming wedding. He declined. He never liked my parents, so I chalked it up to that. My parents have always been loved by my friends, so my fiancé not liking them should have gotten my attention more than it did. Love is so blind, and love and low self-esteem are a dangerous mix. On the Friday night of the concert, I went with my parents. I was sitting next to my dad, and certain words of a song struck me, and I began to cry. I knew. I knew at that moment that I couldn't continue this charade any longer. I leaned over to my dad and told him I needed to tell him and my mom something on our way home. I was very nervous and scared that they would be disappointed in me. As we drove home, I told them that I couldn't marry Kyle. Much to my surprise, the air was filled with relief from all three of us. Come to find out, they had always disliked him. I was crying and sharing my fear of disappointing them. We began speaking about logistics and how to handle the situation with the bridesmaid dresses and canceling the florist and the cake. When I mentioned canceling the church, my dad said in all seriousness, "That was a hard date to get. Don't cancel the church yet. You might meet someone by then." My mom and I looked at each other and laughter erupted.

When I got home that night, I made the call that had been a long time coming. I asked Kyle if I could drive up that night to talk to him. He said it was too late and asked what could be so important. I told him it needed to be a face-to-face conversation. We made plans for me to come up the next day. I had such a mix of emotions and cried frequently that day. As I began the drive, I listened to empowering music and knew that I had to call off the wedding. When I got to his apartment, we hugged and sat on the couch. I shared that I wasn't happy and that I imagined he wasn't happy either. I told him I couldn't marry him. I took the ring off, and the look on his face was one of horror. My heart broke. I didn't want to hurt him. No matter the sadness I had felt in the relationship, this did not feel good. He begged me to stay, to think it over and change my mind. I told him I had done nothing but think about it for months and it had taken that long to get up the courage to share my feelings. He had no idea how far gone I already was. We were both sobbing. I hugged him and walked out the door. I cried all the way home. When I got home my parents hugged me and I cried more. It was a relief, but a very emotional one.

I wish it hadn't been the case, but my self-esteem was so low that I needed the affections from Drew to build me up so I could muster the courage to call off the unhealthy relationship I was in with Kyle. Drew was my safety net. I did not share this detail with Kyle. Things hadn't been working, even before Drew was a factor. Drew was a catalyst for this difficult turning point. I am not proud that this was the path I took, but I have forgiven myself and recognized that it was part of my journey to become the better version of myself that I am today.

5

❖⬥❖

LEAVING THINGS BEHIND

I completed my last internship and graduation requirements. I was able to apply for and accept work as an occupational therapist (OT) if I was being supervised. I was ready to start a new chapter and there was nothing holding me in Portland. I accepted a job as a traveling OT in a small town near where Drew lived. I was enthusiastic and drove out to my first OT job and new life. Things were going well. I liked work, met new friends, and most importantly, I was close to Drew. We looked at houses and talked about our dreams. My three-month assignment became nine months long due to the need for a therapist and the inability to find someone permanent. As the end of my assignment approached, I needed to look for my next job. I tried to find full-time work closer to Drew, but nothing panned out. I got hired by another traveling company to complete an assignment at a children's hospital in the South. I was excited about the prospect, but Drew was not. He took it as a sign that I was giving up on the relationship or wasn't serious about it. That wasn't the case at all. I needed to work, and in my mind, the assignment was temporary. I was still planning to settle near Drew as soon as I could find a full-time job.

I settled into my new assignment and knew immediately that my niche was working with children. The job was right up my alley and my coworkers were great. We did a lot together and took many weekend trips. Drew came to visit me, and we had great plans for the weekend, but they were cut short when he told me he was breaking up with me. I was surprised and heartbroken. He stayed the weekend and we talked about it, but his mind was made up. He wanted to keep in touch and told me that, once I was done soul-searching, if I wanted to move near him, maybe things could get back on track. Little did I know, he had his own "support system" back home.

I thought Drew was the love of my life. I continued my life, but I was heartbroken. He called me about a month later, but I wasn't home. He left a message and called again and again. When we did talk on the phone, he questioned me about where I had been when he had previously called. *Wait a minute. He's the one who broke up with me.* Over the next week he started calling more, and it was clear he had changed his mind about breaking up. This was never clearer than when he surprised me by showing up on my doorstep the next weekend. My parents were in town visiting me, so it made things awkward. After all, everyone knew we were broken up—everyone, that is, except for Drew. It was nice having him back in my life. I loved him and never understood why we had broken up in the first place. We resumed our relationship. At the end of this work assignment, I arranged another assignment so I would be closer to Drew. Drew and I continued dating, but in late spring, I began having a gut feeling that something wasn't right. I talked to Drew about it, and he assured me that everything was fine, but my body told me differently. One day, I was at work, and I couldn't get the unsettling feeling and thoughts off my mind. I felt my heart and mind racing, and it was hard to breathe. I later realized that I had had a panic attack. Each time I alluded to the fact that I thought Drew was cheating on me, he dismissed it. He came to visit me that next weekend and I was a physical and emotional mess. I was seeking reassurance of his fidelity and he gave me lip service, but it didn't suffice. We went for a hike on Saturday and the words Drew was saying didn't match my gut feeling that he was being unfaithful. I remember him driving my car slowly and I got out of the car several times; I was very upset. He was trying to calm me down, and he must have eventually, because I got in the car and we went back to my apartment. Several weeks later, we flew home for my brother's college graduation. I was a frazzled mess. Anxiety had taken over my life and I didn't know how to handle it. It had not come to a head like this before. I felt panicky all the time and I didn't have control over my thoughts. I considered taking my life, and I told Drew I was thinking about this drastic choice. Drew tried to remain calm, but I brought up my suspicions every chance I could. We made it through the graduation, and we were walking from dinner through campus when I just started running. Drew came running after me. I wanted him to chase me, and at the same time, I didn't. I didn't know what I was feeling. Where was this coming from? I had never felt or acted like this. On the drive back to Portland the next day, I was inconsolable and felt out of control in my body. My parents, with Drew's support, checked me into an inpatient mental health facility.

Whether or not it was articulated during my stay, I describe what happened as a nervous breakdown. That week was a range of very extreme emotions. Drew stayed in town for an extra night before heading back home. Each time I tried to call him; he didn't answer. I felt lost. They medicated me in the hospital to calm me, and I went to therapy sessions. I didn't know what was going on. My parents were supportive and visited me daily. I was full of shame. I had my whole future ahead of me, and here I was in a mental ward and couldn't control my emotions. I wasn't sure how this happened or how to correct it.

When I got out of the hospital, I went back home with my parents to heal. Drew and I talked almost every day, and although I felt his support, I still had my suspicions about his authenticity. I went to weekly therapy sessions and to a medication manager who tried to figure out which medicine I needed. I was very resistant to the idea of taking medicine. I felt that if I took medicine, I would be admitting that something was wrong with me. I thought I could fight this on my own. I could overpower this anxiety and depression, or whatever it was that was happening to me. After all, it was situational, right?

I didn't turn to God, who is the only one who could have helped me. I truly believe that God allowed this part of my journey, as a way to bring me closer to Him and closer to doing His will in my life. Unfortunately, I am a slow learner in that department.

I had good moments and many sad moments as I was healing and trying to figure everything out. Drew and I were still dating. He took the stand of staying by my side through this, even if it was only through his words.

6

WHAT COMES AROUND GOES AROUND

One night, I called Drew, and he wasn't home. I felt the need to talk to him, so I looked up the number of a local sports bar he often visited with friends. When I called and asked for him, the waitress on the other end said, "Who is this?" I replied, "His girlfriend." She said, "That can't be. I'm his girlfriend." I hung up the phone.

I called Drew's home number and left a message relaying what had occurred and stated that our relationship was over. He was cheating on me. Everything I had been feeling had been spot-on. This discovery made it easy for me to blame my incidents, my hospitalization, and my anxiety and depression on Drew. It took me a while to get better, but it was easier to do when I could convince myself that he was solely responsible. He tried to contact me several times, but I had cut all ties with him and started to move on.

I wasn't back in Portland for too long when the children's hospital where I had worked called me and asked me to do another traveling assignment to cover a maternity leave. My parents were nervous about me leaving so soon, but it was the fresh start I needed. The start date was a month out. That gave me time to take a vacation with my mom and continue to heal emotionally. I reconnected with my friends and coworkers I had met earlier that year. Within a few weeks I was having symptoms, including stomach pain and blood in my stool. I went to the doctor, and after two appointments and a procedure, I was diagnosed with ulcerative colitis. My emotional stress had taken a toll on my body.

I moved back home to Portland after my assignment concluded. I did contract OT work while looking for a full-time job. A few months later, I was hired by a local school district and started my local career. I was living with my parents, healing, and saving money.

I dated some, but nothing serious. Eventually, I reconnected with a guy I had gone to grade school with. We saw each other in church a couple of times, and once we took time to talk to each other, we clicked. He asked me out and we began dating. I was hesitant and untrusting. He was loving, funny, and patient. It wasn't until I went out of town for a friend's wedding, and I missed him that I realized that I was becoming serious about Emerson.

7

$\diamond\!\!\!\!\!\times\!\!\!\!\!\diamond$

A HEALTHIER LOVE

Things were looking up. I was settling into my new job, and Emerson and I started talking about a future together. The depression and anxiety were still part of me, but they were dormant. I was on a high. I felt fulfilled at work and I was falling in love. After almost a year of dating, Emerson and I took a trip for a work conference, and he proposed. I was filled with excitement and joy, and I immediately said yes. We called our parents, and the celebration and wedding planning began. This time my response and joy were natural and spontaneous.

I was up-front with Emerson about my past, specifically my encounter with anxiety and depression. I honestly think we both thought that he could love me out of it. And for a while, it seemed to work. Emerson was accepting of me, and we had deep, meaningful conversations. I knew he truly loved me, and I loved him. My parents liked him, and he became part of the family long before we were married. We often went to dinner and events with my parents, and I really liked that they enjoyed each other's company. I remember that I had one episode where I became extremely upset and anxious while we were dating, but it didn't seem to faze Emerson. How could it be that I had found someone who loved me despite my flaws? He just wrapped his arms around me and assured me everything was going to be okay.

In the fall of 2001, Emerson and I were married. Despite getting over the flu, it was a beautiful and wonderful day. I had gotten the stomach flu two days before the wedding. I was on the tail end of it, but I still had to consciously focus on not getting sick during the ceremony. By the second day of the honeymoon, I felt completely healed. The day before the wedding, my mom asked me if I was sick or if I was just nervous and getting cold feet. I responded by saying, "I already called one wedding off. If I was this nervous about marrying Emerson, I would have called it off months ago." We both laughed.

We honeymooned and then returned to life in Portland. Emerson had been working for his family business for the past two years after leaving the police force. He had dreams of becoming a CIA agent, so he studied criminal justice and started stair stepping his way toward that career. The police work required changing shifts every three months, which didn't work well with Emerson's need for routine.

We had a good first year of marriage, and I was managing my anxiety and depression okay, but they started rearing their ugly heads again. Emerson was very affectionate with me and was always there for me. Looking back, I'm sure this was hard on him, but he never shared or showed it.

Emerson and I traveled a lot, which has always been a passion of mine. Often, we traveled with my parents, and we always had a lot of fun. I was thriving at work and making my mark. I have always been a high achiever, worked toward goals, and been motivated by praise and accolades. What I would learn later is that my external motivation for success was reflective of my deep-seated low self-esteem and would prove to be unhealthy in many respects. In addition to working as an OT, I became a yoga teacher and tried my hand at writing.

8

✦⊷✧⊶✦

THE STIGMA

I am a friendly, outgoing, and social person. I like to be with people and do fun things. The flip side of this is that I often feel judged or left out, and I often wonder what people think of me. Emerson and I often got together with friends, and I also made time to be with my girlfriends. At times, I backed out of commitments. This became more prevalent in my late twenties and into my thirties. There were times, too many times, when I would commit to something, and when it came around, I would cancel my plans. It was never due to the plans or the people, it was strictly internal. There was something pulling me to stay home and cancel. Its name was depression. I found myself questioning myself and my decisions a lot. From the outside looking in, I had an idyllic life: great husband, great family, great job, etc. The problem was that the monster within me was awakening. I had these intense feelings of sadness that I couldn't escape and didn't understand. The medicine I was on was slowly fading in effectiveness. I looked into seeing a counselor again. I got up each morning and made a day of it, but underneath I felt like I was barely surviving. I would come home, cry, and pull the covers over my head. There were times when I prayed that I wouldn't wake up. *Why God? Why me? Why am I so sad? Why can't I fix this?* These questions made the depression and anxiety spiral downward rapidly. I had a lot of guilt for feeling so sad when I had so much. It didn't make sense to me, and I couldn't accept it. I had many friends, but very few knew of my struggles because I felt ashamed and didn't share. I was ashamed of associating myself with a mental illness. I thought that I could overcome my anxiety and depression on my own. I resigned myself to believing that they couldn't be permanent. At some level I must have believed that if I pretended it wasn't there it would simply disappear. What happened instead was that things became more intense and more stressful. Emerson was supportive, but when I was sad and anxious to the point that I was out of control, he didn't know what to do.

I had many appointments with the nurse practitioner who managed my medication, but to no avail. First she increased the dose of medicine that had worked for five years and then suddenly stopped working. After that failed, she had me try several medications over a long period of time. Nothing seemed to help, and I felt like a guinea pig. I never liked the idea of taking medicine in the first place. After all, taking medication for depression and anxiety cemented the idea that mental illness was a part of me. I could not accept that. After a while, the nurse practitioner started exploring other diagnoses besides anxiety and depression. The thought of something more severe did not help my already fragile state. There was discussion about cyclothymia, which is a milder form of bipolar disorder. She had me chart my moods and episodes on a calendar to see if there were peaks and valleys which would indicate manic episodes and the opposite. During that time she had me try medicine for cyclothymia, but it didn't help me, and after many months, she determined that I did not have any form of bipolar disorder. For whatever reason, my body had acclimated to the medicine that I had successfully taken for five years, and there wasn't anything that seemed to help beyond that.

In the midst of the medication trials, I started going to a chiropractor to address my chronic tension and neck and back pain. I was still dealing with my ulcerative colitis and went through a period when it was uncontrollable. Fortunately, I found a doctor whose approach was a mix of Western medicine and a holistic approach, and my ulcerative colitis has been under control ever since.

9

❀❖❀

NOT ABOUT ME

Things started to take a turn for the worst with Emerson and his job. He wasn't feeling fulfilled and would often reflect on how he had imagined his career path unfolding differently than what he was experiencing. He talked about it occasionally, but more often, he would internalize his feelings of disappointment and failure.

I was concerned about Emerson and his well-being. I rose to the occasion and took the role of caregiver. I don't know if it was due to adrenaline, survival, or a combination of both, but Emerson and his recovery back to health was my only focus. I didn't slip into depression during this time, and I'm still not sure why or how.

Emerson viewed what he went through as situational, but knowing him, I saw it as years of emotional buildup that had been internalized and was finally bubbling to the surface. Eventually, Emerson embraced this to be true as well, but it took a while to get there. Initially, he blamed me and the stress of living with someone who had depression and anxiety. I was very hurt and resented the accusation. I couldn't have imagined what it was like for him to stand by me like he did, but I couldn't choose how he handled things. It was easier for him to blame me than to face his issues.

10

⁜

MOVING FORWARD

Life slowly settled back down. The next June, I found out that I was pregnant. We had talked about having children for a while. I had always loved children, but I was worried about being a mother of a child with a disability. Previously, Emerson and I had met with our parish priest about this, and the priest asked me, "Don't you love the children you work with?" I answered with a resounding yes. He said, "Well, it is only human nature that you will love your own child even more, regardless of any potential challenges." He was right, and I was overthinking. When I found out I was pregnant, I was elated. I was excited to tell Emerson. We were both happy and anticipated the next chapter of our lives together.

I had severe morning, noon, and night sickness during the first several months of my pregnancy. I lost weight and the doctor had to give me treatments to prevent any more vomiting. As I approached the end of my second trimester, I was feeling good. We were busy with our jobs and getting the nursery ready, and we were overall content. About halfway through my second trimester, I started having times when I felt down, but it was nothing overshadowing. As I entered the third trimester, these periods of depression and hopelessness increased. I shared this with my doctor during a regularly scheduled visit for the pregnancy. She offered to put me on medication, but I declined because I didn't want it to affect the baby. A few weeks went by, and the depression was in full swing and I was finding it hard to function. At the next visit, she prescribed me a medicine that she guaranteed was safe and wouldn't affect the baby, especially since I was in the third trimester. If the medicine helped, it was minimal or a placebo effect.

Emerson and I grew closer when I was pregnant. I remember feeling really connected and loved by him. Some of the more special memories were when Emerson and I would occasionally go to the adoration chapel at church while I was pregnant. I prayed for our baby and for our family, and I felt God's presence and it brought me peace.

11

⬦◇⬦

THE NEXT GENERATION

Emerson, my parents, and I went to mass and dinner. After dinner, Emerson and I went to the hospital to check in for the night. The induction was scheduled since I was two days overdue. I feared the labor and the pain. The nurse gave me medicine to induce labor and I went to sleep. When I woke up the next morning, I had some pain but it was not what I had expected. When the doctor checked, I was only dilated to one centimeter, and I was given Pitocin. Contractions started, but the baby didn't move; only its heart rate increased. When they gave me more Pitocin, nothing changed but the baby's heart rate. The doctor didn't want to take any chances, so she decided to do an emergency C-section. During the C-section it was clear by the doctor's actions and words that the delivery was atypical. The baby was under my ribs, and the doctor's traditional techniques weren't working. I'm glad Emerson didn't faint when the doctor told the baby, "Come out already." After many attempts, the doctor switched approaches and used a vacuum to draw the baby out from under my rib cage. Avery was born, and my life has never been the same. Emerson and I were overcome with emotion at the sight of this beautiful little miracle. Our families flooded the room to get a peek at their first grandchild, nephew, great-grandchild, etc. He was the first baby of his generation for both sides of our family, and he was loved.

We went home three days later. I had six months at home with

Avery before I had to return to work. I healed well from the C-section and enjoyed spending time with my baby boy. I had been informed that I was at a higher risk for postpartum depression, so when it came, I wasn't surprised. It wasn't any different than what I had experienced before, but now I had someone else to take care of other than myself. I remember reading Brooke Shields's book about her journey with postpartum depression. It was a wonderful book and it made me feel like I wasn't alone. I was relieved when I read it because my experience was different, and I felt like I had a mild case of postpartum depression. I never felt detached from Avery or had unloving thoughts. I was sad and at times felt restless, but I was—and continue to be—an engaged, caring, and loving mom.

12

꧁ ❖ ꧂

GOD ENTERS IN

Do not fear: I am with you; do not be anxious: I am
your God. I will strengthen you, I will help you, I will
uphold you with my victorious hand. —Isaiah 41:10

E merson and I were both raised Catholic, practiced our faith, and
went to mass together. We prayed together sometimes before meals
and at some other times, but God was not at the center of our lives. For
a few years up until this point, I was faith-searching. I went to retreats,
joined a social justice class, and went on a mission trip. They all brought
me closer to God, and when Avery entered the world, I recognized him
as a miraculous gift from God. I reflected often on the miracle of his
birth and prayed in thanksgiving that we had been blessed and gifted
with such a beautiful responsibility of raising our boy. God was clearly
in my life, but I missed so many obvious times when He was right
beside me or carrying me. For most of my life, I gave myself credit
for my accolades, educational accomplishments, and other things that
happened in my life. I would say, like many other people, that God had
a plan and He doesn't give anyone something they can't handle, but I
didn't apply that to my life. I was too busy trying to control everything.
I was fighting off my depression with the wrong weapons, taking the
lead in my marriage with the viewpoint of "my way or the highway," and
complaining, judging, and blaming others when my feelings got hurt.

My main focal point was Avery, and when I first suspected he might have developmental delays, I went into high gear. He was already the center of my life, and from that moment on, I focused on getting him all of the interventions he needed and carrying through his programming at home. Looking back, I wish I had had the clarity to ask God to step in at that time. Trusting God and turning my worries about Avery to Him and knowing and trusting in His divine providence would have made a difference. Unfortunately, I was far from that place. My anxiety fueled my days. I look back now and am amazed that I was able to function. I loved my baby with my entire heart, and I could tell in the way he looked at me and by his contentment that he felt loved. This was God.

When Avery was almost a year old, Emerson lost his job. Now there were two anxious and depressed people in the house. Emerson continued to sadden as time went on. I added financial insecurity to my list of worries. We grew apart. I expressed my resentment that I had to return to work full-time instead of doing the part-time work I had counted on and the stay-at-home mom role I had been hoping for. I was much less than the wife I intended and wanted to be, but I didn't feel that then.

In the midst of this I continued searching for God, searching for wholeness, and searching for peace and calm. I signed up for a women's retreat called Christ Renews His Parish when Avery was three years old. This was the catalyst for the beginning of my true healing, for my faith life, and for my true relationship with God. It was a weekend where women trusted in God and shared their intimate faith journeys that touched me in a very profound way. I cried throughout the entire weekend. When I was invited to a follow-up meeting regarding a continuation opportunity, I decided not to go. There was my attempt to control again. I decided not to go, but God had other plans. Over that next week He softened my heart, and I answered the call. I had so much guilt and shame built up inside of me, and when I was in this safe space with trusting women who were as vulnerable as I was, my pain bubbled and flowed out of me. I was very scared to share my "faith story" because I was so broken. I didn't know God or how to have a relationship with Him like several of the other women in my group.

The time came for me to share, and my fears of being judged and of not being accepted didn't come to fruition. What? I shared the worst parts of me, and these women, Jesus in disguise, loved me through it. I wasn't alone, and all that I had hidden for years was out in the open and my healing began. After six months, my group had the opportunity to host a retreat for a new group of women. The group discerned that I was to share my faith "witness." I felt called to my ministry, but I was terrified. This was the church where Emerson and I had grown up, and there were bound to be women at the weekend retreat who knew my parents, his parents, or worse yet, his mom could attend. Due to putting much shame around my mental health battle, I had shared this part of myself with very few people, often only out of necessity. Most of my friends didn't know and my in-laws certainly didn't know. This was the time. I needed to trust God and let His will be done. As I stepped to the podium, a calm swept over me and I shared. I cried, shared, and cried some more. I remember the hugs and affirmations I received after I faced my fears, and I felt relief and a release. One of the most healing moments of the weekend was when I had two women approach me separately and tell me that they knew they had been called to the weekend retreat to hear my story. My story. My story mattered. I was accepted and I was helping other women. As healing and wonderful as the retreat process was, I was still very much in a self-centered place and still blamed Emerson for everything. God was working on me, and I was finally open to letting Him in. I started praying more and reading the Bible.

13

GLASS HALF EMPTY

E merson found work, and that brought security for about two years until he was laid off and we were in the same position we had been in with the first job loss. I was very focused on things of this world, and this was compounded by the remaining anger and resentment I had felt from the first job loss. I put my expectations on Emerson and how the job search should look. When his process didn't meet my criteria, it increased my anxiety and my negative opinion of him and his work ethic. I lost respect for him and focused on his flaws instead of his strengths. We were recovering from the first job loss and beginning to get on our feet again and add to our savings. I felt financially insecure and I lacked trust in God. I prayed and talked to God when it was convenient for me or when I felt I was at rock bottom. I didn't realize God was with me and our family at every moment. I had the delusional thought that if I believed in God and prayed, everything would turn out good and would work out in the way I wanted it to. My mantra was "My will be done," not "God's will be done." I was grasping for control, and things were not going well. I was treading water and barely keeping my head above the surface. All of my remaining hopes of being a stay-at-home mom were off the table, and my resentment toward Emerson was at an all-time high. I was selfish and prideful. Emerson had more time at home with Avery, and it was a beautiful thing for their relationship, but I didn't focus on that. I wanted to be with Avery, and instead, I had to pick up more hours at work. I continued to focus on the negative, letting it fester, all the while trying to keep a smile on my face.

14

✣⬦✣

SMILING ON THE OUTSIDE, HURTING ON THE INSIDE

Let us always meet each other with a smile, for
the smile is the beginning of love.
—Mother Teresa

I have always been an energetic and loving person. I smile and laugh a lot. This persona does not match up with my depression. I have occasionally wondered, *Is this a facade? How can I smile and feel so dead inside at times?* In my contemplation, I invited my inner critic to let loose. Over time, I have concluded that there is nothing fake about me or my welcoming smile and bubbly personality. It is God. It is God who is shining through me in those moments. It is God who has gifted me with those qualities to get through the tough stuff. When I have revealed my battle with depression over the years to a few close friends, they each were in disbelief because of my outward persona. If anything, it was quite isolating to have my happy exterior not match up with the hurt I felt inside. No one can know your inner struggle unless you share it with them. That is very difficult to do when you are ashamed of and haven't come to terms with the fact that you have a mental illness. I was caught up in the fear that I wouldn't be accepted and that I would be judged as "crazy" if I shared my true self.

There are mixed messages in our society. The reality and gravity of mental illness is present in our society, but the stigma remains. I can't tell you how many times I have cringed when someone has said, "She's crazy," or, "He's nuts." Heck, I know I say those things without realizing it. These are simple phrases and are not intended to cause harm, but they always give me pause because I think, *That is me*, or, *What if someone thinks that about me?* I believed that if people knew my story, they would think I'm crazy and wouldn't want to be around me.

The teen suicide rate is astronomical. It seems like kids are turning to this permanent solution at younger ages than ever before. There are wonderful efforts being made to end the stigma and reach out to these kids, but what if they don't know how to accept the help or how to be honest with themselves and others? What if they are like me, and they do their best to survive in public but in private their demons haunt them? That makes the challenge of identifying those teens who are most in danger of self-harm because they are hiding their real selves because they are ashamed and embarrassed of who they are. I have heard too many stories of kids who have taken their lives, and their parents were in shock and saw no warning signs. What is scary is that when a person is in a deep depression, there is no rational thinking. At least that has been the case for me. Although there were many good things in my life each time I was thinking the unthinkable, in those moments, I was in a dark cloud that didn't seem to have an end. I don't have a solution, but I pray that no person feels hopeless enough or alone enough to think that taking their life is the answer. I am hopeful that more and more people will speak up about, write about, and sing about mental illness to help people feel accepted and loved, no matter what their circumstances might be. One of the main reasons I pursued writing this book was to potentially reach and help someone who is battling depression. It is important for an increasing number of people to be courageous and share parts—or all of—their journeys related to mental health. The more this exposure happens, and the more the veil is pulled back from the truth of mental illness, the closer we will be as a society to eradicating the stigma.

15

DEFICIENCY MINDSET

Avery was full of energy and joy. My life was centered around him. I was worried about his delays, and I focused on them and what I could do to help him. I looked at it as being proactive, which was true, but now I realize I was overly focused on his delays, and this exacerbated my anxiety. As time went on and more was revealed about the scope of Avery's delays, I wondered what I had done wrong. It had to be something I did. I reflected on my pregnancy and everything I had done or not done up until the present time. I shed a lot of tears on this issue, and to no avail. Nothing changed, other than that my anxiety and depression increased. Emerson reassured me and said, "Avery is blessed to have you as a mom because you know what to do to help him." I agree resoundingly now, but only half-heartedly at that moment. Time went on, and I was wearing my mom and therapist hats full-time at home. We played and I provided all I could to help Avery in his development. This included reaching out to community supports and resources. By this time, Avery was in preschool and was getting the support he needed at home and in the community. I wish I could have accepted Avery wholeheartedly for the blessing and miracle he was and could have seen everything as an opportunity and blessing instead of as a deficit which elicited fear about the future. I projected my fears onto him. It's interesting because, as an OT, I work with families and always focus on the positive and growth in a situation. I couldn't consistently do this with my own son. Now, when I dissect the situation, I can recognize that I wasn't able to—or chose not to—hand everything over to God. God created Avery. He wanted everything, the very best for him, but that hadn't entered into my consciousness. I was his mom, and it was my job to fix, to teach, and to control as much as I could. I can now see this disordered thinking for what it was, but that was the place I was in.

16

⊹◇⊹

DOUBLE DOSE

Things settled into a new normal when Emerson found work. About a year later, we decided to move locally so we could get settled into a new house before Avery started kindergarten. We joined a new parish, and I was craving God and connection more than ever. When the Christ Renews His Parish retreat was offered at our new parish, I felt called. Typically, this is a one-time retreat, but I felt God calling me, and after I got the priest's blessing, I signed up to attend again. This time, I knew the format, but it wasn't less impactful. I was at a different place in my faith journey. I thought I had been healed more than I was. I convinced myself that I wouldn't cry on the weekend like I had a few years prior. Ha! I remember trying to control the tears and the sobbing at different points during the weekend, instead of accepting that this was part of my healing. Shame and guilt die hard. I am so thankful that I had the opportunity to continue my faith journey in this community setting and build my connection not only with God but also with like-minded, God-loving women. Once again, I found myself surrounded by accepting and loving women who were examples of great faith in great trials at different points in their lives. I was discerned to share my story with another group of women. The shame and guilt trickled in as I wrote the draft of my story. I decided to write my faith journey from scratch. There was such healing in writing it out and processing what to share and what to leave out. I noticed that over the past three years of letting God into my life, I had been able to focus more on my faith journey versus my life journey. I was beginning to see where God was in my life from the beginning and where He had saved me. I experienced acceptance and love as I once again shared a part of myself with my faith friends. All those dirty, sinful, unlovable, and shameful parts of me didn't deter these women from loving me as a child of God, just as I was. I started learning how to forgive myself. I began to go to confession more and felt God forgiving me. I was holding on tightly to my sins and all the damage they had done. I gripped at control, and fear rushed in each time I contemplated confession and going face-to-face with a priest. I feared being judged. It was hard enough for me to face my sins, and I did not yet have the humility to sit with a priest, look him in the eyes, and share my deepest, darkest mistakes and sins. Pride is a deadly sin, and it overshadowed my life. Pride is still something I battle with daily. I have made great strides, but each day presents its own challenges. One thing was and is clear: God is and has to be in charge of my life. That is what He wants and what I want, but pride and fear prevent me from handing everything over to Him. There are days when I feel so connected to God and my choices are aligned with His will. Then, just like that, the next day I fall flat on my face. The key for me is to keep focused on Him and ask for His help instead of thinking I can do it without Him. It is so easy for me to spiral into self-pity and depression and the mindset that I won't and can't make progress. In the moments of God's grace, I feel Him wrapping me in His love and know that even with all my failings and sins, there is nothing He can't do, even with a sinner like me.

I have stayed connected with the women who went through this journey with me, and they are still great examples of faith and living a life of striving to glorify God. The sense of community and acceptance is very healing to me. When you struggle to accept yourself, allowing yourself to be open enough to truly reciprocal friendship is a very real challenge.

17

❖❖❖

CONNECTION/NOT GOOD ENOUGH

The facts that God chose me and that I am a child of God had been repeated so often that I started to believe them and let them resonate within my being. Those moments of connection empowered me to take risks, step out of my comfort zone, and be my true self. If only the truth and realization of God's power and my purpose were always anchored within me. Those unanchored times when my self-doubt, past habits, and harmful ways of thinking creep in are detrimental. For as long as I can remember, I've had low self-esteem. I overthink things and judge myself and others too quickly according to my value system at the time. I've had great friendships over my life, but I have always second-guessed my value as a friend. I have had a tendency to connect with someone and lay my heart out and then have sharer's remorse. I start doubting myself and withdrawing from fear of being judged. At the same time, the longing to be surrounded by friends, to be admired, needed, and loved kept nagging at me. Often, I felt like an outsider who didn't belong in a variety of situations. I remember praying on many occasions for the sense of community and to belong. The need to be included was great and is still present to some degree. I'm not sure where this belief and fear of not being accepted came from, but they have manifested in different ways over the years. There are times when I am in a situation and I'm outgoing, conversational, and engaging. There are other times when I am more of an observer, introverted and self-doubting.

18

✢⟡✢

EXPLAIN IT ALL AWAY: HASHIMOTO'S DISEASE

At this point, God was an active part of my life, but so were my depression and anxiety. I had peaks and valleys and sought out talk therapy again. I had formed a trusting relationship with my therapist and was very honest with him about my current state of feeling down often. He asked me if I had ever had my estrogen level tested. "No," I said, "but I happen to have my annual appointment with my ob-gyn tomorrow." There are no coincidences, only God's providence. When I went to my ob-gyn and told her about my therapist's suggestion, she agreed to test my estrogen level but didn't think that it would be a contributing factor to my chronic depression. My doctor followed up with a life-changing suggestion. "Have you ever had thyroid testing done?" I replied that I had, but my T4 level had been within normal limits. "Let's test your thyroid levels." My thyroid-stimulating hormone (TSH) level was 17.0 milliunits per liter (mU/L), which indicated hypothyroidism. The normal range for TSH is 0.4 to 4.0 mU/L. A referral to an endocrinologist followed, as did the diagnosis of Hashimoto's disease. As I learned about the symptoms of hypothyroidism, it was easy for me to convince myself that Hashimoto's had been the cause for my depression all along.

Symptoms of Hashimoto's disease may be mild at first or can take years to develop. Symptoms of an underactive thyroid and Hashimoto's may include weight gain, fatigue, depression, paleness or puffiness of the face, joint and muscle pain, slowed heart rate, constipation, irregular or heavy menstrual periods, and/or a goiter in the throat. I actively had two symptoms at the time (depression and muscle pain), but that was enough for me to advocate that Hashimoto's had been the one and only culprit of my mood disorder over the past many years. I was still fighting the label of a mental health disorder and jumped at the chance to explain it away. It took several months to find the correct level of levothyroxine, but when the doctor did, the dark clouds lifted. I went through a cycle ranging from happiness and feeling better to having feelings of anger because no one had suggested to test my thyroid sooner. I questioned why thyroid testing wasn't mandatory to rule out mental health disorders. The cause of Hashimoto's is unknown, but many professionals suggest that genetics and stress play a role. Hashimoto's was now the second autoimmune disorder I had. I had resigned myself to the fact that stress triggered or caused my ulcerative colitis. After all, it surfaced after the most stressful, traumatic period in my life at that point. It was very possible that my anxiety and stress levels and the way I handled stress had taken on the physical manifestation of Hashimoto's disease. At this point in my life I sought answers to everything. Although I was actively seeking God, I had not yet handed over the reins of complete control. We often think that we have control over situations, when the truth is that we've never been in control of anything. I was fighting God. I refused to accept my crosses and the situations in my life. I didn't want to accept anything that could reflect poorly on me or potentially be negatively received by others. So, when my depression resurfaced a couple of years later, my relief of not having a mental health disorder was challenged and defeated once again.

19

✦⟡✦

HERE'S A PILL

As I came to grips with the fact that I had chronic depression and anxiety, there was still a part of me that wanted a quick fix. In addition to using pure essential oils, which I'll discuss more in a later chapter, I tried acupuncture and Chinese herbs before I came to the realization that I needed to seek out medication again. It had been several years since I had taken medication, and I was resistant because of how they had made me feel like a guinea pig, but it was getting to the point that most of my days felt dark and I didn't feel like myself. I was venturing down the negative paths of guilt and shame. Why was I feeling so down when I was so blessed in my life? Every time I tried a new technique or suggestion, the more I hoped it would be the answer. I was thinking in "all or nothing" terms. The nurse practitioner I had used in the past had moved, so I went to a recommended psychiatrist. The doctor was nice but had focused on medication, which was not my preference. I thought I had been doing fairly well overall, but when she immediately told me I was clinically depressed, I broke down in tears. She prescribed Zoloft. After a month or so, I began feeling better, but I was gaining weight quickly. At my next appointment she said that weight gain was a common side effect. I explained to her that being overweight wasn't helpful for my depression and was a concern. She then prescribed a stimulant to address the weight gain. This was not a rabbit hole I was willing to go down. I left with the prescription for the stimulant and threw it in the trash when I got home. I weaned off the Zoloft safely and was soon back to square one. Square one with twenty extra pounds in six months. I was hesitant to try another drug when I had already tried so many in the past, and I didn't want to gain any more weight. Prior to going to the psychiatrist, I thought I had been doing okay and was holding my own. An insightful doctor once reflected that when you live with chronic depression, your reality is skewed and your "okay" is not typical. People get used to their realities, and their perceptions are framed from significant sad and dark moments, so when you aren't experiencing the intense sadness, things may seem normal. Time passed and I coped and went on with life as best I could. My depression didn't quit, and some phases of my life were more difficult than others. After some time, I made an appointment with my primary-care doctor and inquired about the next steps to take in treating my depression. I shared about my recent experience and my hesitancy to go to another psychiatrist. He suggested that I try Effexor again. I was apprehensive because, although it had been helpful for five years, it had stopped working. The doctor shared, "Sometimes, when you take a break from a medicine and try it again, the chemistry works again in the brain and body." I didn't understand the science, but I trusted him, so I left with a prescription—and for me, his suggestion worked. The Effexor was effective and continues to be so for me presently.

20

UNDISCOVERED TRAUMA

There are many types of trauma, and I have seen clients on a regular basis who have dealt with trauma of some kind. Professionally, I began to learn about trauma-informed teaching and therapy, the effects of trauma on learning, and effective strategies to help my clients. As I began to learn for the benefit of others, things began stirring within me. The book, *The Body Keeps the Score*, by Dr. Bessel van der Kolk was the tipping point and the catalyst for seeking healing from my personal traumas. As I read his book, certain markers that indicate childhood trauma and/or abuse resonated with me. I had always found it puzzling that I didn't remember much of my childhood. As I read about disassociation and how some people "forget" their traumas as a coping mechanism, only for them to manifest physically, I wondered. I wondered because a distant memory, most likely based on a story I had been told several times, had popped into my thoughts every now and then for as long as I could remember. *Could I have been abused and didn't remember? Could that be why I didn't remember most of my childhood? Is that why I engaged in self-injurious behaviors in my early twenties during the period of my nervous breakdown? Could it be? Or was this another attempt to explain away my depression and anxiety and not take ownership that this was a part of me?* I prayed a lot, and then it was time for action. I was most interested in pursuing eye movement desensitization and reprocessing (EMDR), to see if I could dismiss or validate my childhood trauma.

Source

1. Van Der Kolk, B. A. (2014). *The Body Keeps the Score: Brain, Mind, and Body in the Healing of Trauma.* (7th ed.). Viking.

21

❖❖❖

MAKE-BELIEVE OR MEMORY

W as there a way to discover if there was truth to my suspicions? Is this why many past strategies had been lacking to some degree? What was leading me down this path?

During my intake with the social worker I was referred to, she shared that there were different types of trauma. There are two main categories of trauma commonly referred to as "big T" and "little t" traumas. "Big T" traumas are the events most commonly associated with post-traumatic stress disorder (PTSD), including serious injury, sexual violence, or life-threatening experiences. Threats of serious physical injury, death, or sexual violence can cause intense trauma even if the person is never physically harmed. "Little t" traumas are highly distressing events that affect an individual on a personal level but don't fall into the "big T" category. Examples of "little t" traumas include non-life-threatening injuries, emotional abuse, bullying or harassment, and loss of significant relationships. "Little t" traumas can be extremely upsetting and can cause significant emotional damage. This is especially true if an individual experiences more than one traumatic event, or if these traumas occur during important periods of brain development like in early childhood and/or adolescence. The social worker identified several things I shared with her as "little t" traumas, and they needed to be processed. She said there might be a repressed "big T" trauma, but there was no guarantee it would be revealed. I proceeded to seek out the EMDR therapy to see if processing my "little t" and possible "big T" traumas would help me heal from the inside out. I will discuss more about EMDR in a later chapter.

22

$\ast\!\!\!-\!\!\!\diamondsuit\!\!\!-\!\!\!\ast$

SEEKING AND COPING

We humans are social creatures, and we seek connection. We long to be accepted and loved. It is fascinating to examine the habits and vices people will develop when those needs aren't met on some level. It is normal to seek and want friendship, love, and connection. I took a wrong turn when I focused on worldly connections instead of seeking a connection and friendship with God. In my adult life, I have tried to fill my "God-sized hole" with unhealthy relationships, adventures, technology, and food. Some of these habits have been extremely difficult to break. I have God and faith on my side, but I often forget to turn to Him in my moments of seeking and need. I have learned many wonderful strategies that bring me closer to God when I exercise them and seek Him out. Learning how to cope with disappointments and unexpected and/or uncomfortable life situations takes a lot of work. I have found solace in true connection with authentic people who accept me despite my flaws. I continue to push through times of discomfort when my flaws come to mind and encourage myself to seek connection. It is always worth the risk, but taking the risk can be overwhelming and challenging, especially during times when I'm focused on my flaws rather than my gifts and positive attributes.

Building and continuing authentic friendships is an ongoing journey for me and one I want more than anything. I have several people whom I would consider to be close friends, and I know I could share anything with them, and they would be there for me in any circumstance. These are friends who know my story, my struggles, and my strengths. They are encouraging, fun, and real. There are times within these friendships when my internal critic gets the best of me and I begin to have doubts about myself. *Am I good enough?* I seek and long for close friendships, but at times, my insecurities will surface when I think about my friends having deeper connections with others. I realize how petty and unrealistic this is, and I've spent a lot of time evaluating where this comes from. I am hopeful that my friends don't notice, but there are times when I realize my actions or thoughts are coming from a place of insecurity and because I am seeking reassurance from my friends of my value to them. There are times when I know and feel my identity as a beautiful daughter of God. I want this knowledge to settle into my bones and my soul so deeply that my confidence and self-worth come from this identity. It is when I begin to compare myself to others or when I doubt myself that my insecurities surface. I continue to pray for true connections and friendships with God-loving and faith-filled women. God has already answered this prayer in so many ways and so many times, especially over the last decade. My newer prayer is for the grace and strength to accept myself for who I am in any situation, including in social settings. I pray that I can live as my authentic self, regardless of my menacing self-doubt and insecurities that often try to creep in and disrupt my growing self-love, self-acceptance, and confidence.

I pray that I am able to let go of any remaining unhealthy friendships that make me doubt who I am and bring about internal doubt and shame. I choose to focus on my friends who emulate faith and are on the same God-seeking path as I am. I pray that I will always accept and love myself, even when others evidently don't. I strive to wholeheartedly want the best for every human, even those who have—and will— hurt me.

23

TO JUDGE OR TO BE JUDGED

If you judge people, you have no time to love them.
—Mother Teresa

Over time, I had developed the defense mechanism of judging others to protect myself. I didn't realize I did this until my therapist identified that I do this to protect myself from the pain of being judged. He said it's very common but judging creates a barrier so that a person doesn't look within for healing, but instead, faults others to make themselves appear more whole. I had never thought of myself as a judgmental person, but as I reflected on what he said, it started to make sense. I was so afraid of being judged and piling on others' negative opinions of me to my own self-loathing, that I put this harmful protective layer around myself. I wasn't capable of delving into the self-love and inner child work that I clearly needed to do. I didn't even recognize this judgmental pattern in myself, not to mention how detrimental it was to my spirit and to others.

24

❖◇❖

FIGHT OR FLIGHT

Stress responses are part of our biology and often keep us out of danger. The problem occurs when a person gets stuck in a stress state (fight, flight, or freeze). A person can get stuck in a stress state when the brain and body are unable to naturally process the trauma. As our bodies are constantly experiencing stress, it is as if the trauma continues to happen whether we are conscious of it or not. The trauma can manifest in the body and be the cause of emotional and/or physical disease.

I had been in a stress state for decades and had no idea this was the case, until recently. I realize now that I was fluctuating between fight, flight, and freeze states and was very seldom ever in a place of true calm or status quo. This explains my jumpiness and why I would often feel on edge and would easily be triggered or startled. Many of my decisions and emotional responses came from this frightened place. I am much more mindful of my state of mind now, and I often catch myself becoming tense and ready to react out of fear.

25

SHINING THE LIGHT ON SHAME

Shame has overshadowed most of my life, and I am done. I have learned that when I have the courage to share those parts of me that I am afraid to share, they have less power over me. Keeping painful memories and choices inside allows them to fester and continue to cause damage. Every time I get past my fear and don't succumb to the feelings of shame, whatever they might be in the moment, I step into the light and grow in the right direction. I tell my son all the time that there is nothing he could ever do that would make me love him less. If it's true for me as a mother, how much more does God feel that way for me and for each one of us? We are His children, and He doesn't want us to stop coming to Him because we made a mistake, even if it was a significant one. God wants us to turn toward Him and trust Him.

There have been many situations when I've made a decision out of fear or shame. It's a pattern that has been a part of me, but I have learned that it doesn't have to be this way. When fear or shame are in my heart, I have learned to pause and offer it in prayer. At times, I sit with the feelings, and this can be painful, but it is much less painful than the effects of letting fear control your life. Often, the feelings of shame and fear have been so great that I didn't think they would ever dissipate, but they did. Sitting with difficult emotions and contemplating where the feelings are coming from can dissipate their negative pull and power and allow you to gain insight into why you were feeling that way in the first place.

I'm not sure when or why it started, but I had been in the pattern of judging and shaming myself for almost everything. I wanted to be accepted and to fit in and have everyone like me. I catered to what I thought people wanted instead of taking the time to decide what was the right thing to do and the best thing for my well-being. If I acted rashly or immaturely, I guarantee that memory haunted me, and I didn't or couldn't forgive myself for being human. I held myself to a higher standard than I would ever hold anyone else to. I apologized too often, and so often, that it naturally became my response even when it didn't fit the situation.

Learning to give myself grace and to forgive myself for past mistakes has been difficult. I know God has forgiven me for my past sins and mistakes that I have confessed, but it is often more challenging for me to forgive myself. I have worked hard to not let the opinions of others influence my decisions to do what is right for me in general and in particular situations. I used to tie what others thought of me to my self-worth. This is a dangerous scenario and one that contributed to my many downward spirals into depression.

I am becoming strong enough to accept who I am and live from a place of authentic self and truth, regardless of whether I'm accepted. As I have been on this path, I have connected with many true friends who share the same values and support me and love me for who I am. I can now assert myself and feel confident in who I am because I am focused on God and His ways and truth instead of focusing on the world. I had been confused for a long time; I was drawn to the darkness, and I buried myself in shame by trying to get approval from certain people. It is not important what others think of me or you. The importance comes from living your authentic truth, and I believe this comes from letting God lead your life.

As I have embraced living my faith, I have encountered many naysayers and people who are on different journeys. In the past, this would have caused me to doubt myself and would have stirred up thoughts of shame and sadness of not fitting in. I am different now. I realize that I am not meant to fit in with everyone. I am meant to be the best example of love and kindness to everyone I encounter, and if I'm not their cup of tea, that's okay. I have come to terms with others who think differently than I do. It helps tremendously that I have surrounded myself with friends who have the same morals and life goals that I do. This helps me to feel very supported and loved, just as I am. When I have days when fear and shame creep in, I have many tools and strategies that I can use to ward off the unhealthy and unwanted thoughts.

We were not meant to live in fear and shame. We were not meant to journey alone. We are meant for connection with others and to seek goodness and holiness. If you are feeling fearful or shameful about something, don't believe the lies. You are meant to thrive and not to be held back by a veil of darkness. If you have never sought help from a therapist and you feel like you have significant issues to overcome, that is a great place to start. You were made in the likeness and image of God. Thinking anything else is false and will lead you down the wrong path.

26

❖◇❖

PUZZLE PIECES

Throughout my journey and battle with my depression and anxiety, I have found some effective strategies. Initially, I had hoped that each one would be the cure-all, but time proved that this wasn't realistic. Looking back, I was seeking a fix instead of accepting and embracing all parts of me. I continued to view myself as broken and not enough. I felt that I needed to keep adding things or trying things to change my situation. This can be a positive mindset, but I was coming from a place of not accepting and loving myself for who I was at my core. There are several things that I have discovered and learned along the way that have supported my health and well-being. I use the analogy of looking at myself and my struggles as a puzzle, and each strategy or therapy I try is a puzzle piece. Some fit perfectly and some don't fit at all. At first, some may seem to fit, but then I may realize that they don't belong in that part of the puzzle or maybe they don't fit in my puzzle at all. The following chapters are resources for you. I am sharing them to let you know that you are not alone and to bring hope if you are feeling stuck or frustrated on your journey toward healing. Don't be discouraged if some aren't up your alley or if you've tried some and they weren't right for you. I encourage you to look at this as trial and error. Keep what works for as long as it serves you and pass by the rest.

27

✦⬧✦

PRAYER AND FAITH

Some people are born into faith and have that connection from a young age. For many, they were raised a certain way and have fallen away from those beliefs for a multitude of reasons. For others, they go through the motions of a certain faith but don't truly feel connected to a higher power. There are still others who find God through trauma, negative circumstances, or when they've hit rock bottom. I personally can relate to the last three at some points in my life.

Regardless of your belief or nonbelief, I encourage you to continue reading. Open your heart and mind to these shared ideas and prayers that you can use and adapt them for your journey. Please be open to the notion that you are reading this book at this time and place in your life for a specific reason. There is something drawing you to search and seek for something, and just maybe, it's connecting with God.

My most important friendship must be with God, and everything in my life must flow from this relationship if I truly want to feel joy and be fulfilled. This statement is true, but I have struggled to live it for many years. I have often let busyness and distractions interrupt or replace my prayer time. When I pray, especially quiet prayer, my heart is often full and I feel the presence of God and/or the Holy Spirit. In the past, I have had grandiose plans of getting up early and doing daily meditation and prayer first thing each day, just to hit the snooze button instead. This has happened more times than I can count. Prayer must be a commitment, and commitment takes work. It takes showing up even when you don't want to or when ten other things are vying for your attention. I've had periods of time when I have shown up for daily quiet prayer and have reaped many benefits, but then I move on before it becomes a habit. In my mind and heart, I want God to be the center of my life, but my execution of living a life for God often, if not always, falls short.

I have learned many methods of prayer and specific prayers that have helped me on my faith journey. I continue to battle distractions and spiritual laziness as I learn more about my faith and earnestly pray and commit to spending more time with God daily.

The following pages have ideas and examples of forms of prayer. There are many more options than I mention here, but these are the ones that are on my heart to share:

- Traditional prayers related to specific religions carry history and meaning. They can be helpful in connecting to your higher power and source. In my Catholic faith, some examples are the "Our Father," "Hail Mary," and prayer before meals and bed.

- Arrow prayers are thoughts you send up throughout the day.

- Intercessory prayers are those that are prayed on behalf of other people. When we pray with the intention of helping others, God hears us. There is great power in prayer. We are called to pray even for those who hurt us. This is very challenging yet has tremendous healing power.

- *Lectio divina* is a form of prayer in which you read a portion of Scripture three times with a specific intention each time. One way to summarize this form of prayer is: "read, relate, reflect."

  o   Read: Read the Scripture passage aloud the first time.

o Relate: When you read it the second time, look for a word or phrase that you can relate to or that catches your attention.

o Reflect: The third time you read it, let the words resonate with you, and sit and reflect with what comes to your mind and to your heart.

- The Rosary is a historical tradition in the Catholic Church. Through many apparitions over time, Mother Mary has stated the importance of the Rosary and its power to change circumstances and history. The Rosary consists of opening prayers, then five decades which consist of one "Our Father," ten "Hail Marys," one "Glory Be," and the "Fatima prayer." The mysteries are meditations to reflect upon as one prays the Rosary on beads. There are the sorrowful, glorious, luminous, and joyful mysteries which all consist of Jesus's life and His sacrifice for our sins.

  o The Holy Family School of Faith is an organization based in Kansas that challenges its members and others to pray the Rosary daily. They provide a podcast with meditations before each decade based on theology, the history of the Catholic Church, the sacraments, and more. Praying the Rosary daily by listening to the podcast has helped me understand my faith at a deeper level.

    ▪ For more information about the Holy Family School of Faith and the Rosary movement, please visit https://www.schooloffaith.com.

- Silent prayer is arguably the most important and difficult form of prayer. In silent prayer, one chooses to open their heart and sit at the feet of God and let His grace and mercy penetrate their heart. For me, distractions seem endless on most days. It is my choice to spend time with God and attempt to clear my mind and open my heart to Him that allows Him to come to me. He wants my yes and your yes. He wants us to approach Him and be with Him, as a friend and companion. He wants us to listen and grow in His love. Consider starting with five minutes per day. As you continue to choose silent prayer, you will begin to crave this quiet time and connection with God. Allow yourself to carve out up to thirty minutes a day for silent prayer.

- Adoration is a beautiful tradition in the Catholic Church in which the body of Christ is present in the Eucharist in a monstrance, most often in a chapel or in a dedicated space. I have been doing an adoration hour weekly, on and off, for many years. Adoration can be a form of silent prayer. It is choosing to spend time with God and asking for His will to be done in your life. It is letting God know your gratitude and that you choose Him to guide your life.

- Singing is a beautiful form of prayer. This doesn't need to be limited to church. There are many Christian music stations, in addition to songs that many mainstream artists have written and performed that glorify God. You don't have to have a good voice to sing. Let the spirit overtake you. One of my teachers once told me that when singing reaches Heaven, it all turns into angelic tones. Let's hope so in my case.

- The "Divine Mercy Chaplet" came out of visions and guidance that St. Faustina received from Jesus in the early twentieth century. The chaplet is prayed using the beads of the rosary.

    1. Make the sign of the cross.

        a. "In the name of the Father, and of the Son, and of the Holy Spirit. Amen."

2. "You expired, Jesus, but the source of life gushed forth for souls, and the ocean of mercy opened up for the whole world. O, fount of life, unfathomable divine mercy, envelop the whole world and empty Yourself out upon us."

3. "O, blood and water, which gushed forth from the heart of Jesus as a fount of mercy for us, I trust in You." (Repeat three times.)

4. "Our Father, Who art in Heaven, hallowed be Thy name; Thy kingdom come; Thy will be done on earth as it is in Heaven. Give us this day our daily bread; and forgive us our trespasses as we forgive those who trespass against us; and lead us not into temptation but deliver us from evil. Amen."

5. "Hail Mary, full of grace. The Lord is with thee. Blessed art thou amongst women, and blessed is the fruit of thy womb, Jesus. Holy Mary, mother of God, pray for us sinners, now and at the hour of our death. Amen."

6. The Apostles' Creed: "I believe in God, the Father Almighty, Creator of Heaven and earth, and in Jesus Christ, His only Son, our Lord, who was conceived by the Holy Spirit, born of the Virgin Mary, suffered under Pontius Pilate, was crucified, died, and was buried; He descended into hell; on the third day He rose again from the dead; He ascended into Heaven, and is seated at the right hand of God, the Father Almighty; from there He will come to judge the living and the dead. I believe in the Holy Spirit, the holy Catholic Church, the communion of saints, the forgiveness of sins, the resurrection of the body, and life everlasting. Amen."

7. On the decade bead, pray: "Eternal Father, I offer You the body and blood, soul and divinity of Your dearly beloved

Son, our Lord, Jesus Christ, in atonement for our sins and those of the whole world."

8. On the ten small beads of each decade, pray: "For the sake of His sorrowful passion, have mercy on us and on the whole world."

9. Repeat steps seven and eight for the remaining decades, saying the "Eternal Father" on the "Our Father" bead, and then "For the sake of His sorrowful passion" on the following "Hail Mary" beads.

10. "Holy God, holy Mighty One, holy Immortal One, have mercy on us and on the whole world." (Repeat three times.)

11. "Eternal God, in whom mercy is endless and the treasury of compassion inexhaustible, look kindly upon us and increase Your mercy in us, that in difficult moments we might not despair nor become despondent, but with great confidence submit ourselves to Your holy will, which is love and mercy itself."

- *Visio divina* is similar to *lectio divina* but uses an image instead of the Scripture. Choose a religious, spiritual, or other meaningful image upon which to pray. Find a quiet area to settle in with the image in front of you. There are many ways to engage in *visio divina*. I am sharing the way in which I was taught below. If this form of prayer resonates with you, I encourage you to seek out variations to find the one that best meets your needs.

  o Gaze at the image, focus on what first catches your attention, and let it speak to you. You can keep your eyes on the image or rest your eyes, keeping the image in your mind's eye.

  o The second time you look at the image, gaze upon the entirety of the image. Allow the grand scheme of the image to invoke a word or an emotion. What questions arise? What is the Holy Spirit or God revealing to you?

o When you are ready, open your eyes and gaze upon the image a third time. Imagine that you are in the image. What do you see, hear, smell, feel, or taste? Reflect with all of your senses. Pray as emotions, questions, words, and thoughts come to you. After you have gazed at the image for several minutes, close your eyes and continue to pray. Rest in God's presence.

• Bible diving is a technique in which you randomly open the Bible and read where your eyes guide you. This act often affirms to me that there are no coincidences and God will guide what I need to read at that moment.

• There are many novenas and prayers that may call to you. Some of my favorites are the "Litany of Trust" and the "Litany of Humility."

• Technology can help you access the faith through apps on your phone or in daily emails. Some of my favorites are:

o The Laudate app

▪ You can access many prayers, novenas, and information about the faith on this free app.

o Regnum Christi daily meditations

▪ Sign up to get these sent to you via email daily.

▪ They are short and succinct and share the gospel reading for the day, as well as reflection and a suggested daily resolution.

o   Dynamic Catholic daily reflection

- Sign up to get these daily reflections in your mailbox.

- This organization also has options to sign up to receive daily emails during Lent and Advent to deepen your faith.

Source

1. "How to Recite the Chaplet," *The Divine Mercy*, https://www.thedivinemercy.org/message/devotions/pray-the-chaplet

2. "Visio Divina," *Prayer + Possibilities*, https://www.prayerandpossibilities.com/pray-with-eyes-of-the-heart-visio-divina/

28

✤❖✤

SCRIPTURE

Your word is a lamp for my feet, a light for my path.
—Psalms 119:105

G od speaks through Scripture. The Bible is divinely inspired, and
every word is guided by the Holy Spirit. I have often heard that
BIBLE is an acronym meaning: basic instructions before leaving earth.
I grew up hearing Scripture read in church, but it did not occur to me
to read the Bible on my own. Over the last decade, I have embraced
Scripture and allowed it to guide me and comfort me when I most
need it. Below are some of my favorite verses and the common reasons
I selected specific Scripture that have brought me hope and peace in
uncertain times.

When I'm feeling anxious ...

- Cast all your worries upon him because he cares for you. (1
  Peter 5:7)

- Trust in the LORD with all your heart; on your own intelligence
  do not rely; In all your ways be mindful of Him, and He will
  make straight your paths. (Proverbs 3:5–6)

- Have no anxiety at all, but in everything, by prayer and petition, with thanksgiving, make your requests known to God. Then the peace of God that surpasses all understanding will guard your hearts and minds in Christ Jesus. (Philippians 4:6–7)

- When I am afraid, in You I place my trust. I praise the word of God; I trust in God, I do not fear. (Psalms 56:4–5)

- Do not fear: I am with you; do not be anxious: I am your God. I will strengthen you, I will help you, I will uphold you with my victorious right hand. (Isaiah 41:10)

When I'm feeling sad or discouraged ...

- Come to me, all you who labor and are burdened, and I will give you rest. (Matthew 11:28)

- Even though I walk through the valley of the shadow of death, I will fear no evil, for You are with me; Your rod and Your staff comfort me. (Psalms 23:4)

- No trial has come to you but what is human. God is faithful and will not let you be tried beyond your strength; but with the trial He will also provide a way out, so that you may be able to bear it. (1 Corinthians 10:13)

When I'm feeling thankful ...

- Rejoice always. Pray without ceasing. In all circumstances give thanks, for this is the will of God for you in Christ Jesus. (1 Thessalonians 5:16–18)

- Give thanks to the Lord, who is good, whose mercy endures forever. (Psalms 106:1)

- The Lord is my strength and my shield, in whom my heart trusts. I am helped, so my heart rejoices; with my song I praise Him. (Psalms 28:7)

When I'm feeling hurt ...

- The Lord will fight for you; you have only to keep still. (Exodus 14:14)

- God is our refuge and our strength, an ever-present help in distress. (Psalms 46:2)

When I know I need to forgive, but it's really difficult ...

- Be kind to one another, compassionate, forgiving one another as God has forgiven you in Christ. (Ephesians 4:32)

- But I say to you, love your enemies, and pray for those who persecute you, that you may be children of your heavenly Father ... (Matthew 5:44)

- Finally, brothers, whatever is true, whatever is honorable, whatever is just, whatever is pure, whatever is lovely, whatever is gracious, if there is any excellence and if there is anything worthy of praise, think about these things. Keep on doing what you have learned and received and heard and seen in me. Then the God of peace will be with you. (Philippians 4:8–9)

When I'm tired or I feel like giving up ...

- He gives power to the faint, abundant strength to the weak. (Isaiah 40:29)

- I have the strength for everything through Him who empowers me. (Philippians 4:13)

- The valiant one whose steps are guided by the Lord, who will delight in His way, may stumble, but he will never fall, for the Lord holds his hand. (Psalms 37:23–24)

- Rejoice in hope, endure in affliction, persevere in prayer. (Romans 12:12)

- For I will slake the thirst of the faint; the appetite of all the weary I will satisfy. (Jeremiah 31:25)

- Let us not grow tired of doing good, for in due time we shall reap our harvest, if we do not give up. (Galatians 6:9)

When I'm facing a challenge …

- Jesus looked at them and said, "For human beings this is impossible, but for God all things are possible." (Matthew 19:26)

- My soul, be at rest in God alone, from whom comes my hope. (Psalms 62:6)

When I'm feeling distracted …

- Let your eyes look straight ahead and your gaze be focused forward. (Proverbs 4:25)

- In all your ways be mindful of Him, and He will make straight your paths. (Proverbs 3:6)

29

✦⟡✦

SAINTLY FRIENDS

May today there be peace within. May you trust God
that you are exactly where you are meant to be. May
you not forget the infinite possibilities that are born of
faith. May you use those gifts that you have received
and pass on the love that has been given to you. May
you be content knowing you are a child of God. Let
this presence settle into your bones, and allow your
soul the freedom to sing, dance, praise and love. It is
there for each and every one of us.
—St. Teresa of Ávila

Intercession of the saints is something that I have used a lot over the
past several years as I've increased my knowledge of specific saints.
I turn to the saints because they each have walked the path of faith,
many among and despite difficulties. They turned to God and had a
childlike dependency on Him in all circumstances. Ask the saints to
pray for you. They were real people who walked different journeys but
ultimately chose God and answered the call to be holy saints, like we
are all called to do. They are examples of what I strive to be. As I write
this, I realize I need to tap into their intercessory powers all the more.

If you don't believe in the power of the saints and aren't ready to
pray for their intercession, that's okay. Acknowledge that they were real

people and walked upon the earth as you and I do. Allow them to be examples of goodness, grace, and love inspired by God. Look at the saints individually and select ones that inspire you in your life. Learn their stories, the prayers they used, and other signature things about them that purified them and helped them become better people each day.

Many saints are the patrons of one or more things. For example, St. Anthony is the patron saint of finding lost things, and St. Francis of Assisi is the patron saint of animals. Depending on your situation and what you are seeking, there is most likely a saint or saints who can relate to that topic or situation.

St. Dymphna is the patron saint of mental illness. I often turn to her and ask for her intercession on difficult days. A formal prayer to St. Dymphna is below.

> Lord God, who had graciously chosen Saint Dymphna to be the patroness of those afflicted with mental and nervous disorders and has caused her to be an inspiration and a symbol of charity to the many who invoke her intercession, grant through the prayers of this pure, youthful martyr, relief and consolation to all who suffer from these disturbances, and especially to those for whom we now pray. (Mention your specific request.) We beg You to accept and grant the prayers of St. Dymphna on our behalf. Grant to those we have particularly recommended patience in their sufferings and resignation to Your divine will. Fill them with hope, and if it is according to Your divine plan, bestow upon them the cure they so earnestly desire. Grant this through Christ, our Lord. Amen.

I most often ask for Saint Dymphna's help at night before I go to bed. Most of the time, my prayer is informal as I ask for her intercession for strength, courage, and perseverance on my rough days.

In addition to St. Dymphna, I often ask for the intercession of St. Joseph, Mother Mary, St. Jude, St. Monica, and St. Mother Teresa. I enjoy learning about the stories of the saints. As I think about the saints, I realize how far I must go to become the person God willed me to be, but I am thankful He gave me examples of people who surrendered to His will and allowed His grace to pour into their lives.

Mother Teresa draws me in. I cannot fathom the depth of her love of God as evidenced by her twentieth-century example of unconditional love. She surrendered her will and her preferences and allowed God to work through her and impact millions of lives for the better. I bring Mother Teresa up because she is current. She is known in our world, and she made a tangible difference. I pray often for her intercession to increase my humility and charity and to soften my heart. Which saint do you identify with?

Source

1. "St. Dymphna-Saints & Angels" *Catholic Online*, https://www.catholic.org/saints/saint.php?_id=222

30

❖◇❖

EYE MOVEMENT DESENSITIZATION AND REPROCESSING (EMDR)

Eye movement desensitization and reprocessing (EMDR) was discovered and developed by Francine Shapiro, PhD, in 1987 to help people process traumatic memories. The emphasis in EMDR is to allow the information processing system of the brain to make the needed internal connections to resolve the emotional disturbance.

EMDR is noninvasive, and the client is in charge of the direction and pace of the session. Talking in detail about the traumatic event or issue is not needed, which was a relief to me. The client is asked to hold an image or event in mind while the bilateral stimulation occurs. Through the eight phases of EMDR the client learns how to be present with the trauma, notice how it affects their physical and emotional body, as well as replace negative patterns and thoughts with positive beliefs. The certified therapist facilitates the process and is trained to help the client safely navigate and process the trauma.

Processing the trauma means setting up a safe internal state that allows experiences that are causing problems to be integrated and stored appropriately in your brain. That means that what is useful to you from an experience will be learned and stored with appropriate emotions in your brain, and what is harmful will be released. The inappropriate emotions, beliefs, and body sensations will be discarded. Negative emotions, feelings, and behaviors are generally caused by unresolved earlier experiences that are pushing you in the wrong directions. The goal of EMDR therapy is to leave you with the emotions, understandings, and perspectives that will lead to healthy and useful behaviors and interactions.

While reading *The Body Keeps the Score* by Dr. van der Kolk, I learned more about EMDR therapy. I had a friend who did it a few years ago and it helped her, but I didn't know much more than that. As I read and researched, I decided that EMDR therapy was worth seeking out to try and resolve any unprocessed or unidentified trauma.

I made an appointment with my psychologist. I was hesitant to share my questions and thoughts for fear of being thought of as crazy, but something inside urged me to take the chance. As I shared the signs that I personally related to of child abuse and trauma, she validated me and said it was worth exploring. She also shared that my patterns of difficulties that I had discussed previously with her matched with a history of trauma.

I met with my EMDR therapist weekly for fifty-minute sessions. My therapist made me feel comfortable and explained a little more about EMDR and what our sessions would look like. During the second session it was time to proceed with the bilateral stimulation and tackle the first trauma. My therapist showed me a technique to do self-tapping, and at other times, I held a device in each hand that alternated pulses while I envisioned the past event or parts of the event. Through the course of each session I was asked to evaluate if and where I felt tension or the trauma in my body and how strongly I felt the trauma or positive belief, depending on the phase I was in during the EMDR therapy.

I was hopeful, yet skeptical, about EMDR and the anecdotal success stories I had heard and read. I became a believer when I was able to sit with an image and thoughts associated with a trauma and be able to be more of an observer rather than being in the scene. I was able to step back in my mind and observe the scene objectively and recognize that it wasn't my identity. It was the first time in twenty years when I thought about some events and didn't feel extremely uncomfortable, wasn't full of shame, and/or didn't burst out in tears. Over the course of four sessions, the therapist led me through the EMDR phases to process the effects of being exposed to pornography in my college relationship and looking at how that had impacted me going forward in my life. During the fourth session I was able to think about that relationship and the uncomfortable moments without shame. Instead, I moved toward the acceptance that those experiences were a part of my life and did not have to define who I am. My therapist was skilled at identifying where to start the therapy. When I mentioned my college relationship and being exposed to pornography, I didn't feel like that was as significant as several other events in my earlier life. I quickly learned that I was stuck in the shame of allowing myself to be in a relationship with someone who saw me and other women as objects. My low self-esteem, need for love and approval, and low level of confidence provided the fuel for me to remain in that relationship much longer than I had wanted to. Through this process I learned that I needed to forgive that old part of me and embrace her and forgive her.

Issue by issue, I processed and healed as I went through the EMDR process facilitated by my therapist. Initially, when I brought up the possibility of having a subconscious trauma, she said it was possible that it could be revealed during EMDR but not a guarantee. I sought out EMDR primarily to validate or dismiss a "big T" trauma, but when the EMDR started, it was clear I had many "little t" traumas to process first. Over the months of therapy I began to feel more complete and whole. Through the EMDR process I discovered and explored several "little t" traumas that have impacted my life and have shaped me. Before this therapy, I often gave less credence to these events and stuffed them down, thinking I could ignore them. I assumed that I had to have endured a "big T" trauma for it to have impacted me in such a way that the trauma indicators I have learned about resonated with me. During my EMDR therapy it was not revealed that a "big T" trauma had occurred in my early childhood. The most educated conclusion I can draw at this time is that the compilation of the "little t" traumas I have experienced throughout my life had a larger impact on me than I had realized.

Trauma is not to be dismissed. Trauma, and the way it affects you neurologically and emotionally, is personal and unique to each person. If you feel that you have endured trauma in utero; during childhood, adolescence, or adulthood; or at any point in your life, I encourage you to explore that and consider ways to release the physical and emotional scars that trauma can cause.

Source

1. "What is EMDR?," *EMDR Institute, Inc.,* https://www.emdr.com/what-is-emdr/

31

✧

ACE IN THE HOLE

As I progressed through EMDR therapy, I continued to learn about trauma and its effect on development. On several occasions over a span of three years, I learned about the ACE study and questionnaire. ACE stands for adverse childhood experiences. The ACE study revealed that there is a significant link between childhood trauma and stress in early life and chronic diseases in adulthood, including heart disease, lung cancer, diabetes, and autoimmune diseases. The study also identified a direct link between the ACE score and emotional and social issues such as depression, domestic violence, and suicide.

The study showed that adverse childhood experiences were more common than had previously been recognized or acknowledged by research and medical findings.

The ACE questionnaire is a ten-item self-report measure developed for the ACE study to identify childhood experiences of abuse and neglect. The higher the ACE score a child or person has, the more at risk they are for physical and mental disorders.

The questionnaire identifies major risk factors that may lead to the development of health and social issues among people in the United States. The questionnaire may be able to help those who have a high ACE score to become more informed about their increased risk factors for health issues. It could also encourage them to seek treatment or therapy if they have not already done so.

Although the questionnaire is not all-encompassing and does not apply to all forms of trauma, it can be helpful to take the ACE questionnaire to bring understanding to your situation or to rule out such experiences as a contributing factor to any mental health issues you may be battling.

To find your own ACE score or learn more about the ACE questionnaire, please visit https://acestoohigh.com/got-your-ace-score/.

Source

1. "Adverse Childhood Experiences (ACEs)," *Center for Disease Control and Prevention,* https://www.cdc.gov/violenceprevention/aces/index.html

32

GRATITUDE AND JOY

The root of joy is gratefulness.
—David Steindl-Rast

Regardless of the current mood or situation, there is always something for which to be grateful. There may be times when it is more difficult to find but developing a habit of detecting and writing down gratitudes provides a shift in perception and focus. There are many ways to practice daily gratitude. I have found that keeping a journal by my bed works well. I write three new gratitudes for each day.

Another fun and motivating way to hold yourself accountable is to have a friend to share these daily gratitudes with. This can be through a quick phone call, text, or email each day. I have enjoyed learning about my friends and their perspectives when I have done this approach to daily gratitude. Requiring yourself to list three new gratitudes can be challenging, but it deepens the awareness of all there is to be grateful for.

You might be thinking this sounds easy, but if you are in a dark place, it might seem unfathomable. Take a deep breath. Give thanks. You made it through that moment. Take another breath. Consider giving thanks for making it through each moment, or each breath, if thinking beyond that is too daunting. There is no wrong place to start. Look around you and within you. There is beauty in light. Begin noticing and begin practicing gratitude for the little things. As you increase your awareness for all the things there are in which to be grateful, there will be less room for the negative.

33

✦◦✧◦✦

THE GRID

I have a tendency to distract myself with activities, projects, and things to do. I often fill my plate too much. I used to view this as being energetic and productive. While this is true, I have identified that I often seek out new and fun activities to fill voids in other areas of my life. It is important to evaluate your patterns, and if something negative is becoming a habit or pattern, consider revisiting how it could change or serve you better.

In thinking about my approach to my commitments and how I often feel when my calendar is overloaded, I decided to use a grid system to help me reflect and reorganize.

Monday	Tuesday	Wednesday	Thursday	Friday	Saturday	Sunday

Monday	Tuesday	Wednesday	Thursday	Friday

Monday	Tuesday	Wednesday	Thursday	Friday	Saturday	Sunday

Monday	Tuesday	Wednesday	Thursday	Friday

Take a look at each of these grids separately and pause for a little bit. Notice your physical and emotional reactions to each grid. Let that guide you in setting parameters as you go forward in planning your days, weeks, and years ahead.

For me, the Monday-through-Friday grid with two slots under each day is the most calming. The Monday-through-Sunday grid with multiple slots makes me feel nervous and unsettled.

Think about the following areas and plug them into a grid (or grids) to see how they feel:

- Family time
- Self-care
- Gardening
- Time with a friend
- Cooking

- Organizing
- Volunteering
- Exercise
- Journaling
- Prayer/meditation

- Time in nature
- Reading
- Phone call/FaceTime
- Unstructured time
- Chores

This is your personal fulfillment grid. This is above and beyond work and your daily responsibilities. How much time are you able and/or willing to schedule for each point above or other areas that come to mind?

Use my examples as a jumping-off point and adjust your activities and grid to suit you—then stick to it. Let it be the boundary to protect your emotional health and your valuable relationships. Whether you select a grid with one or five extra spaces per day, give yourself permission to leave some blank or label them as "Unstructured" to earmark them as time slots to decompress and be in the moment without an agenda.

Below is an example of one of the weekly grids I have created and used. This system allows me to visualize my commitments in a whole-picture perspective and to see in what areas of life those commitments are in. It has been helpful for me to notice where I am spending the most time and where I need to reallocate some of my time.

Monday	Tuesday	Wednesday	Thursday	Friday	Saturday	Sunday
Cooking/ family dinner	Spiritual reading	Family quiet prayer time after dinner	Bio Mat/ quiet time or phone call with friend	Adoration	Exercise	Gardening (weather permitting) or bath with oils
Walk with family or a friend	Yoga with a friend	Volunteer		Exercise	Family time	Cooking/ family dinner

Please keep in mind that when I write something in the grid, I intend to stick to it. Other things can happen during the day; for example, family time happens more often than indicated in the grid. Placement in the grid assures that it happens at the minimum indicated. I am a planner and I like to see things plotted out. This gives me perspective, and I've learned to tune in with how I feel when looking at my weekly schedule so that I can make tweaks accordingly. My schedule is still full, but now my days are more consistently filled with activities that either help others and/or feed my soul and purpose.

34

MEDITATION

I have known about meditation and the acclaimed benefits associated with it for years. I had considered doing a daily meditation practice many times. There was always something that I chose over making meditation into a habit. Each time I tried meditation, my mind wandered and I lost interest. Little did I realize that this was a sign that I needed it all the more. Recently, I have pushed through the discomfort and busyness and made time for daily meditation. I started with five minutes, and now, most days, I meditate for twenty to thirty minutes. There are many approaches to meditation and many types of meditation. Most often, I choose silent prayer meditation at the beginning of the day.

The premise of meditation is to sit comfortably and still in a quiet environment, in which you bring yourself back to the present moment and/or your breath, repeatedly. It may work better for you to lie down comfortably, but I caution you that it might be too easy to fall asleep.

The facts are that meditation:

- Reduces anxiety

- Reduces depression

- Reduces chronic pain

- Reduces the risk of heart disease and high blood pressure

- Increases focus and concentration

- Improves self-awareness and self-esteem

- Lowers stress levels

Progressive Relaxation Meditation

1. Lie down comfortably and close your eyes. (A modification is to sit in a supported seated position.)

2. Begin to focus on your breath and allow your body to melt into the floor.

3. Draw your attention to your feet.

    a. On an inhale, squeeze your left foot and lift it slightly off the floor. On an exhale, gently bring it down and relax your foot.

    b. On an inhale, squeeze your right foot and lift it slightly off the floor. On an exhale, gently bring it down and relax your foot.

4. Bring your awareness to your legs.

    a. On an inhale, lift your left leg slightly off the floor. Activate all your leg muscles. On an exhale, gently release your leg on the ground and let the tension move out of your leg.

    b. On an inhale, lift your right leg slightly off the floor. Activate all your leg muscles. On an exhale, gently release your leg on the ground and let the tension move out of your leg.

5. On an inhale, squeeze your glutes. On an exhale, release into your seat bones and release your glutes.

6. On an inhale, activate and squeeze your core and abdominal muscles. Release your core on an exhale.

7. Bring your attention to your arms.

    a. On your next inhale, lift your left arm slightly off the ground and squeeze your hand into a fist. On your exhale, release your muscles and lower your arm to the floor.

    b. On your next inhale, lift your right arm slightly off the ground and squeeze your hand into a fist. On your exhale, release your muscles and lower your arm to the floor.

8. Inhale and tense the muscles of your back. On an exhale, completely release all the muscles in your back.

9. Lift your head slightly off the floor and engage your neck muscles as you inhale. Gently release your head and neck on an exhale.

10. Bring your attention to your face.

    a. As you inhale, pucker your lips and cheeks, and scrunch your face, engaging all your facial muscles.

    b. As you exhale, release all the muscles of the face and release the tongue to the bottom of your mouth (lower palate).

11. Take several breath cycles and scan your body.

12. When you are ready, on an inhale, engage and activate all the muscles in the body.

13. On an exhale, completely release the tension throughout the body.

    a. Take several breath cycles, focusing on letting go of tension and releasing more and more into the earth.

    b. Release more than you think you can on each exhale.

14. Quiet your mind and allow your focus to be on the natural, uncontrolled breath for several minutes.

    a. Inhale and observe.

    b. Exhale, increase relaxation, and completely let go.

15. Slowly open your eyes and begin to bring gentle movement back into your body.

16. Consider journaling about your meditation experience.

Self-Love Meditation

1. Lie down comfortably and close your eyes. (A modification is to sit in a supported seated position.)

2. Inhale through your nose and exhale through your nose. Gently guide the inhale to the belly, encouraging gentle expansion, and release your belly naturally toward the spine on each exhale.

3. As you inhale, draw in thoughts of love, peace, and acceptance. On each exhale, release any negativity and anything that is preventing you from accepting yourself fully for who you are.

4. Allow your body to soften and relax as you quiet your mind and still your body. Breathe into the stillness and notice what comes up.

   a. If any busy thoughts or agendas come up, gently redirect your attention to your breath without judgment.

5. As emotions or physical sensations or awareness come up, stay with them and breathe into them.

   a. Inhale awareness, exhale letting go of anything that no longer serves you.

6. When you get to a place where you feel calm and settled, begin to breathe into your heart center.

   a. Inhale "I love myself," or, "I accept myself for who I am."

   b. On each exhale, release any resistance or negativity surrounding your view of yourself or a current difficult situation.

   c. Stay with this breathing cycle for as long as needed.

7. On an inhale, bring your hands to your heart and visualize bringing more peace, love, and acceptance into your heart than you have ever known.

   a. Exhale and feel loving and peaceful energy expand from your heart outward into every cell of your being.

    b. Take at least six breath cycles here with your hands on your heart.

8. On your next inhale, hug your knees into your chest and gently roll to the side. If you are seated, gently bring movement back into your fingers and toes.

9. Gently bring yourself into a seated position and open your eyes.

10. Journal about your experience.

Nature Meditation

Nature is a powerful healing agent. Immerse yourself in a calming outdoor setting for the meditation below.

1. Sit or lie down in a comfortable seated position.

    a. Some suggestions include sitting in a chair on a porch, patio, or balcony; lying in the grass; sitting against the base of a tree; or sitting next to the bank of a water source such as a lake or a river.

2. Begin bringing your attention to your breath as you inhale and exhale naturally through your nose.

3. Allow yourself to settle into physical stillness and allow your breath to proceed in its natural rhythm.

4. Begin to awaken your senses to what you hear, smell, and feel around you.

5. Inhale connectedness to the earth and release your body or parts of your body in deeper contact with the earth.

    b. Feel completely supported by the earth.

6. Stay and breathe in this place for several minutes.

    a. If, and when, you become distracted by thoughts, gently acknowledge them and allow them to pass like clouds as you redirect your attention to your breath.

7. Inhale and breathe in the fact that you are connected to the earth and the universe.

    a. Continue the breath cycle, knowing that you are exactly where you need to be at this moment.

    b. Stay here for a few minutes or for at least ten breath cycles.

8. When you are ready, begin to gently bring movement back into your fingers and toes and gently open your eyes.

9. Journal about your experience.

35

THE POWER OF SILENCE

We need to find God, and he cannot be found in
noise and restlessness. God is the friend of silence. See
how nature—trees, flowers, grass—grows in silence;
see the stars, the moon and the sun, how they move
in silence … We need silence to be able to touch souls.
—Mother Teresa

My mind is constantly fluttering with information. When I breathe and try to quiet myself, my mind still races. I have noticed that the more time I quiet myself physically and draw my attention inward or outward to a calming source (such as nature, a diffuser, or a picture), I am able to achieve stillness and a quiet mind. This has been a very slow process for me. Along the way I have been discouraged and have stopped trying at times, but I continue to come back because I know that silence is where I will find peace.

We are constantly inundated by sounds, demands, visual stimuli, and more throughout each day and night. It has become the norm in our society, and our nervous systems and our health suffer. We were not created to be engaged mentally, physically, and visually all the time. When we constantly turn outward toward all these distractions, it becomes more difficult to reflect on what is happening internally. Depending on your journey, it could be very painful to be in silence, to let what is happening inside unfold and to be in that space. Now I recognize that, for years, I had the tendency to busy myself with other commitments and activities to inadvertently avoid the silence because it was too uncomfortable to hear my internal monologue. It gets better. It may not be easy, but it gets better—and you are not alone. Healing starts in the silence.

36

+~◇~+

MIND, BODY, SPIRIT CONNECTION

I am a subscriber to the belief that everything that makes up a person is interconnected. If something affects the body, it also affects the mind and spirit, and vice versa. I tried yoga for the first time when I was in my early twenties, and I continue to practice in some form to this day. When I started practicing yoga, I was primarily focusing on the physical benefits, but it is the calming and mind-healing benefits that have kept me practicing and learning new techniques for more than two decades. I recently realized that I have maintained and expanded my yoga practice because it serves me in many ways. Pranayama—breath work—is the foundation of yoga. It is centering, calming, and organizing. The breath connects the body, mind, and spirit. Focusing on and staying with the flow of the breath allows a person to ride the waves of physical sensations, thoughts, and emotions on and off the mat. Practicing yoga has provided me with a physical outlet while also giving me an internal awareness, increased confidence, strength, and calm. There are many types of yoga and there are benefits to all of them. The opportunity to learn to calm the mind through the breath as sensations come my way has been the pinnacle for me. Thoughts race in and out of my mind all day. They continue to race, sometimes at a faster pace, when I try to turn them off or slow them down. Quieting the mind to be an observer is a feat I have not yet mastered, and some days and practice sessions are more successful than others. I highly recommend starting with a live class with an instructor who is attentive and offers modifications and adaptations. There are many wonderful videos and livestream classes online, but nothing replaces a knowledgeable teacher who can objectively help you reach your goals while ensuring you listen to your body and respect your boundaries.

In the beginning, my idea of a successful practice was being able to do everything the teacher did. During that period I missed out on learning how to listen and honor my body so that it could open and release what was not serving me. I benefited from the physical exercise, but my choice to force my body into poses that didn't come naturally poured tension into my muscles and caused injuries that I am still working on releasing more than twenty years later.

The roots of yoga can be traced back to the Indus-Sarasvati civilization in northern India over five thousand years ago. The word "yoga" was first mentioned in the oldest sacred texts, the *Rig Veda*. Yoga derives from ancient Indian spiritual practices and an explicitly religious element of Hinduism (although yogic practices are also common to Buddhism and Jainism). Yoga is a group of physical, mental, and spiritual practices or disciplines which originated in ancient India. The term "yoga" in the Western world often denotes a modern form of yoga focusing on exercise and consisting largely of postures, or *asanas*.

Yoga philosophy is one of the six major orthodox schools of Hinduism. The yoga school's systematic studies to better oneself physically, mentally, and spiritually have influenced all other schools of Indian philosophy. Yoga gurus from India later introduced yoga to the West. Outside India, it has developed into a posture-based physical fitness, stress-relief, and relaxation technique. Yoga in Indian traditions, however, is more than physical exercise; it has a meditative and spiritual core.

A question I frequently have run into is: "Is yoga a religion?" It's not for me. It is true that its roots are in Hinduism. However, my application of yoga has nothing to do with religion. I practice yoga for the mind-body-breath connection to minimize my anxiety and maximize my peace and calm. I use yoga as a means to stay mentally and physically in tune and fit. I incorporate my Catholic faith and beliefs into my yoga practice whenever possible. Often, when I choose a mantra, it is faith-based, such as, "Let go, let God," or, "Draw near to me, Jesus." Personally, I take the elements of yoga and other health practices and use them for my benefit without attaching religious value to them.

Several people from my church have asked me if I know about Pietra fitness. I have investigated it, and although Pietra fitness claims it is not yoga, from what I understand, Pietra fitness has taken many yoga poses, changed the names, and added Scripture to the exercise sequences or classes. I believe this was developed to break away from any association to yoga's roots in Hinduism. I personally don't see the difference in practicing yoga using the mindset that I do, which is that of being an exercise that benefits my mind, body, and soul.

Whether you are new to yoga or are an experienced yogi, here are some suggestions I have found helpful for my practice:

- Be consistent. Decide if you are going to do it once, twice, or three times a week, and stick to it. Build up to a longer and more substantive practice.

- Start small. It is better to practice for five to ten minutes a day correctly and consistently than to do a practice for a longer period of time inconsistently.

- Variety is the spice of life. Try different poses, flows, and types of yoga until you find what meets your needs and feels right for you in the present.

- Honor your body. Focus on what your body is able to do and breathe gratitude into that space.

- Ask questions. Advocate for yourself and talk to the teacher prior to or after class if you want more information or help with something.

On the following pages you will find unique and original yoga sequences I have created for the purposes of this book. I have recordings of each sequence on my YouTube channel if you prefer to follow along with a teacher.

Yoga Sequence for Calming

In general, forward bending poses are calming for the mind and nervous system. Certain types of pranayama, or intentional breath work, also help to calm and ease anxiety. Below is a sequence designed to support calming and relaxation.

1. Easy Pose (Sukhasana)

2. Forward Fold (Pashchimottanasana)

3. Bound Angle Pose (Baddha Konasana)

4. Downward-Facing Dog (Adho Mukha Svanasana)

5. Standing Forward Bend (Uttanasana)

6. Mountain Pose (Tadasana)

7. Extended Triangle Pose (Utthita Trikonasana)

8. Half Moon Pose (Ardha Chandrasana)

9. Standing Forward Fold (Padangusthasana)

10. Head-to-Knee Forward Bend (Janu Sirsasana)

11. Seated Forward Bend (Pashchimottanasana)

12. Legs-up-the-Wall Pose (Viparita Karani)

Yoga Sequence for Mood Elevation

Chest openers and backbends often have energetic effects and support increased joy and openness.

1. Constructive Rest

2. Bridge Pose (Setu Bandha Sarvangasana)

3. Cat Pose (Marjaryasana) and Cow Pose (Bitilasana)

4. Extended Puppy Pose (Uttana Shishosana)

5. Mountain Pose (Tadasana)

6. Standing Forward Fold (Padangusthasana)

7. Cobra Pose (Bhujangasana)

8. Child's Pose (Balasana)

9. Upward-Facing Dog (Urdhva Mukha Svanasana)

10. Child's Pose (Balasana)

11. Easy Pose (Sukhasana)

12. Seated Twist (Ardha Matsyendrasana)

13. Head-to-Knee Forward Bend (Janu Sirsasana)

14. Relaxation (Savasana)

37

⬥⬥⬥

CHAKRAS

The seven chakras are the main energy centers of the body. "Chakra" means "wheel" in Sanskrit. The chakras are thought to be spinning disks of energy that should stay open and aligned, as they correspond to bundles of nerves, major organs, and areas of our energetic body that affect our emotional and physical well-being. When our chakras are open, energy can run through them freely, and harmony exists between the physical body, mind, and spirit. If chakras get blocked, there may be physical or emotional symptoms related to a particular chakra.

The seven main chakras run along the spine. They start at the root, or base, of the spine and extend to the crown of your head. Many people believe there are more than one hundred chakras in the body.

1. Root Chakra *(Muladhara)*

The root chakra represents our foundation. It is located at the base of the spine. When the root chakra is open, we feel grounded and have a sense of stability. We feel confident in our ability to withstand challenges and stand on our own two feet. When it's blocked, we feel threatened, as if we're standing on unstable ground. Your root chakra is responsible for your sense of security and stability.

Color: Red
Element: Earth

Stone: Hematite

2. Sacral Chakra *(Swadhisthana)*

The sacral chakra is located approximately one to two inches below your belly button. This chakra is responsible for your sexual and creative energies. It's also linked to how you relate to your emotions as well as the emotions of others. Those with a blocked sacral chakra could feel a lack of control in their lives.
Color: Orange
Element: Water
Stone: Tiger's eye

3. Solar Plexus Chakra *(Manipura)*

The solar plexus chakra is located in your stomach area. The third chakra speaks to your ability to be confident and in control of your life. It is related to self-worth, self-esteem, and self-confidence. If your solar plexus chakra is blocked, you might feel overwhelming amounts of shame and self-doubt. Those with open solar plexus chakras are free to express their true selves.
Color: Yellow
Element: Fire
Stone: Amber

4. Heart Chakra *(Anahata)*

The heart chakra is located near your heart, in the center of your chest. The heart chakra is about our ability to love and show compassion. It is the bridge between the lower chakras and the upper chakras. Someone with a blocked heart chakra will have difficulty fully opening up to the people in their life. If someone's heart is open, they can experience deep compassion and empathy.

Color: Green
Element: Air
Stone: Rose quartz

5. Throat Chakra (*Vishuddha*)

The throat chakra gives voice to the heart chakra and controls our ability to communicate our personal power. It controls our ability and comfort with communicating verbally. When the throat chakra is open, it allows us to express ourselves truly and clearly. Someone with a blocked throat chakra may feel like they have trouble finding the words to say how they truly feel.

Color: Light blue/turquoise
Element: Sound/music
Stone: Aquamarine

6. Third-Eye Chakra (*Ajna*)

The third-eye chakra is located between your eyes. It controls our ability to see the big picture and connect to our intuition. It registers information beyond the surface level and is often responsible for our gut instincts. It is also linked to imagination.

Color: Dark blue/purple
Element: Light
Stone: Amethyst

7. Crown Chakra (*Sahasrara*)

The crown chakra sits at the crown or top of the head and is the highest chakra. The crown chakra represents your spiritual connection to yourself, others, and the universe. It also plays a role in your life's purpose. When the crown chakra is open, one can see their inner beauty and they can achieve a higher consciousness.

Color: Violet/white
Element: Divine consciousness
Stone: Clear quartz

Being aware of the chakras has been a source of increasing internal awareness and connection with my mind, body, and spirit. It is helpful for me to focus on a certain feature associated with a specific chakra depending on my mood or when I am faced with circumstances where I need to calm and clear my mind and body.

Chakra Meditation

If you choose to supplement this meditation with stones and/or essential oils, have them available and accessible in the order you would like to use them.

1. Sit or lie down in a comfortable supported position.

2. Bring your attention to your breath and begin to bring your attention to your seat bones.

    a. Visualize red at the base of your spine, where the root chakra is located. Inhale connectedness and grounding through the seat bones.

    b. Breathe in security and comfort.

3. Bring your awareness to the area in the pelvic bowl, between the hip bones.

    a. Visualize an orange disk or circle of light in this area, the sacral chakra.

    b. Breathe into the awareness of how you are feeling. Acknowledge any emotions that come up and stay with them until you are able to release them on an exhale.

4. Bring your attention to the area around and a bit above your navel or belly button. This is the solar plexus chakra.

    a. Visualize the color yellow in this area.

    b. Inhale "I am worthy and enough," or, "I love myself for who I am," or something similar that resonates with you.

    c. On each exhale, release any tension in this area and throughout the body.

5. When you are ready to move on, shift your attention and allow it to rise along the spine to the heart area.

    a. Inhale and exhale as you visualize the color green.

    b. Notice your emotions, and once again, sit with them and allow yourself to accept how you are feeling in this moment.

    c. Inhale love and compassion for yourself and exhale any self-doubt or judgment.

    d. Stay here for several breath cycles, ideally until you feel centered and can sense calm and love radiating from your heart.

6. Bring your attention to your throat area and begin to visualize the color blue.

    a. Breathe in openness and freedom to express yourself in a kind and loving way.

    b. Release any tension in and around the throat, neck, and shoulder areas.

7. Shift your awareness to your third-eye chakra, located between the eyebrows.

    a. Visualize a purple hue with slight blue tones.

    b. Breathe into your innate goodness and intuition. Allow yourself to be trusting of your instincts and release any urge to attempt to control things in this moment.

8. Visualize a white/light purple light at the crown of the head at the crown chakra.

    a. Inhale and feel connected to yourself, others, and the universe.

    b. Exhale, feel your body being supported, and release any remaining tension.

    c. Stay here as you breathe and let your connectedness to everything and everyone resonate within you.

9. Acknowledge any thoughts and gently release them as you draw your attention back to your breath.

    a. Inhale from the root chakra at the base of the spine and slowly up through the spine until you reach the crown chakra.

    b. On each exhale, release from the crown chakra down to the base of the spine.

    c. Breathe into the colors of each chakra as you make your way up and down the spine with the breath and your internal awareness.

    d. After at least six deep breath cycles, allow the breath to return to its natural rhythm.

10. Gently begin to bring movement to the fingers and toes and open your eyes.

    a. Breathe into the openness and release you've created during this meditation.

11. Journal and reflect on your meditation experience.

38

❦⬦❦

ENERGY WORK

Reiki is a Japanese technique for stress reduction and relaxation that also promotes healing (Rand 1999). It is a type of energy healing and correlates with the chakras in the body. Typically, during a Reiki session, the client lies down, relaxes, and breathes while the practitioner works. If nothing else, lying in silence and breathing away from demands is a great start to healing.

I had known about Reiki for years, and it took me ten years and encouragement from a like-minded friend before I stepped out of my comfort zone and took the training. There are many benefits and aspects of Reiki that have supported my healing and my role in helping others heal. Like yoga, Reiki refers to certain entities related to spirituality that I am uncomfortable with and don't subscribe to. I believe it is important to be open to things and to try unfamiliar things because it may be one of those missing puzzle pieces.

From the beginning, I have never blurred the lines of my faith and my religious beliefs. My Reiki training opened me up to the idea of energy work and healing and incorporating them into my practice. I have wrestled with the dilemma of whether it is within the boundaries of my Catholic beliefs for me to practice Reiki. I sought advice from several spiritual mentors and prayed a lot on how and if I can incorporate Reiki into my practice.

To avoid conflict with my Catholic faith, I have decided to hone my craft as faith-filled energy work. When I practice, I invoke the Holy Spirit, Jesus, and Mary, and it is a form of active prayer. There are many charisms of the Holy Spirit, one of which is healing. I am actively practicing this charism and am enjoying connecting with God, prayer, and others in this way. If you are interested in a faith-filled energy session with me (virtually or in person) please contact me at faithfilledwellness@gmail.com.

39

✦◇✦

ESSENCE OF THE EARTH

I was introduced to essential oils and signed up for a starter kit through Young Living eight years ago. I made this investment in search of an all-natural solution to help support my son's needs. Once I received the kit, I quickly realized that these oils can not only benefit my son but also our entire family.

I started researching oils that would help support depression and anxiety, and I began diffusing them, taking baths with them, and putting them on my skin. What works for me may not work for everyone, but there are several oils that have constituents and a chemical makeup that support emotional health and well-being. My go-to oils when I'm feeling down are ylang-ylang, lavender, clary sage, orange, and frankincense.

My personal preference is Young Living essential oils because of their seed-to-seal guarantee and the 100-percent pure nature and transparency of the company. I learned that using Young Living essential oils was more than aromatherapy. Due to the fact that Young Living oils are therapeutic-grade, they have medicinal and healing properties to support all aspects of health: body, mind and spirit. I am actively building my community and team with Young Living. If you are interested, I encourage you to learn more about Young Living and their products. If it is a part of your journey to join my team, I would like to have you in my community. I will have more information about how to join my team (Member #3024687) at the end of this chapter. For now, let's get back to the goodness of the oils.

It took me several years to completely switch from chemical-based products to natural products and pure essential oils. One of the reasons I made this commitment and choice was to decrease the chemical burden in my body (and my family's bodies) that had built up over the years. I had become accustomed to using popular advertised products without even considering if they would be harmful to my health. I fell victim to marketing campaigns and didn't think about what was in the products I was using. Once I learned about the many harmful ingredients in common products I used daily, I knew I needed to switch things up.

Please read the labels on your cosmetics, cleaners, and other household products. While there are many ingredients that are harmless, there are some very dangerous chemicals that are common in products that many people use daily. Repeated exposure to these harmful chemicals creates a chemical burden, indoor air pollution, and can cause health problems.

The FDA does not have much authority regarding regulating chemicals in cosmetics and household products. Many of the chemicals discussed in this chapter are banned in many countries around the world, but the United States is not yet one of them. Harmful chemicals are often found in:

- Cosmetics
- Laundry detergent
- Dryer sheets
- Toothpaste
- Mouthwash
- Antibacterial soap
- Shampoo, conditioner, and other hair products
- Household cleaners
- Air fresheners
- Candles

Many of the above products are either applied to the skin or breathed in. Harmful chemicals in these products enter the bloodstream via the skin and the lungs.

Many of the most harmful and common chemicals to have in your system are listed below.

Chemical	Danger		Chemical	Danger
Phosphates	Heart disease, osteoporosis, death, toxic to marine life		2- Butoxyethanol	Causes liver and kidney damage, throat irritant
Formaldéhyde Paraformaldéhyde Méthylène glycol Quaternium-15	Carcinogen, volatile organic compound (VOC)		Bleach and chlorine	Hormone disruptors, respiratory and skin irritants
Mercury	Can damage kidneys and nervous system		Volatile organic compounds (VOCs): petroleum distillates, limonene, alcohol, and esters	Hazardous chemicals that are linked to cancer and asthma
Parabens	Disrupts hormones, harms reproductive system, carcinogen		Phthalates	Endocrine disruptors, poses risk during prenatal and early postnatal development, carcinogen, harmful to the immune system
Sodium Laureth Sulfate and Sodium Lauryl Sulfate	Skin irritant, can damage internal organs, toxic to environment		Ammonia	Asthma, bronchitis

M- and o-phenylenediamine	Irritates the skin, damages DNA, carcinogen		Synthetic or artificial fragrances and dyes	Chemical sensitivity, allergic reactions, carcinogen, endocrine disruptors
Aspartame	Carcinogen		Benzene	Carcinogen, causes optical damage, highly toxic to marine life
Paraffin wax	Creates highly toxic and carcinogenic fumes when burned		Dioxins	Damage to the immune system and reproductive system, developmental issues

The first step is to realize and become more aware of what ingredients are in the products you and your family are using. Allow yourself time to transition to all-natural and safe products gradually. If you want to take a big step and clean everything out at once, that is amazing. For me, that was too daunting and overwhelming. I needed to take my time to think through the process, research, and become more informed as I made the switch to healthier and natural alternatives.

In addition to using the oils for aromatherapy, I have found functional uses that work great, save money, and are healthy alternatives to chemical-laden products. Here are some of my favorites:

- Lemon oil as a degreaser and sticker remover

- Add lavender, purification, or citrus fresh to dryer balls in the last ten minutes of the drying cycle

- Add frankincense and lavender to shea butter or natural lotion to support skin health

- Add a few drops of purification and thieves to a glass spray bottle for a surface cleaner and room freshener when traveling

- Put thieves oil on the bottoms of your feet to support immunity when you're sick

- Diffuse lemon, peppermint, and lavender during allergy season

- Put peppermint on the top, sides, and/or back of your head when you have a headache (avoid contact with your eyes)

- Put lavender on cuts and scrapes to support healing

- Use peppermint (put on wrists to inhale, and/or on the stomach) to help with motion sickness

- Use tea tree oil on acne

  o Make a face spritz using witch hazel and several drops of tea tree oil

- Add a couple drops of peppermint and/or tea tree to your shampoo to prevent lice

- Use the Thieves cleaning line for all of your household cleaning needs:

  o Laundry

  o Oral hygiene

  o Dishwashing

Using the oils and other natural products has lightened the toxic load on my system and has increased my health and well-being. I feel good about supporting my physical and mental health by avoiding common offender chemicals that can affect my mood and bodily functions.

To learn more, go to https://www.youngliving.com. My member number is 3024687. I look forward to accompanying you on your chemical-free journey.

40

⊹❖⊹

YOU ARE WHAT YOU EAT

For God did not give us a spirit of cowardice but
rather of power and love and self-control.
—2 Timothy 1:7

What goes into your body can—and will—affect your physical
and emotional health. It is important to eat foods that have a
variety of vitamins and minerals. There are many fad diets that people
swear by, but I believe that a balanced diet including many fruits,
vegetables, and proteins is the best route.

Some foods that have been found to decrease anxiety include:
asparagus, avocado, blueberries, turkey, almonds, yogurt, spinach, and
salmon.

If you are anything like me, if you are feeling stressed and/or sad,
you crave carbs and/or sugary foods. While they may satisfy in the
short term, a diet with too many carbs and sugars will contribute to
feeling sluggish. Choosing "smart" carbs,—such as fruits, whole grains,
vegetables, and legumes—can satisfy your cravings, and they have also
been shown to have a calming effect by increasing serotonin, which is a
mood-boosting chemical in the brain. Protein, tryptophan, B vitamins,
vitamin D, selenium, and omega-3 fatty acids have all been identified
as being helpful for supporting a positive mood and natural energy.

I continue to work toward eating healthier and in moderation.

When I am mindful and pray for self-control and focus on God in my weak moments, I find more success than when I try to fight through my invasive thoughts and tendencies on my own. I know that God is trying to do something through me and that this battle is not in vain. It is easy for me to get down on myself when I give in and turn to food. It seems that when I put more pressure on myself to make a certain choice, I am more likely to do the opposite. I logically know what is healthy to eat, but there is something at play other than nutrition here. I will not give up; I will continue to strive to eat a healthier, balanced diet that will best serve my physical and mental health.

Source

1. "Beat Anxiety: 8 Foods That Help with Anxiety and Stress," *Psycom*, https://www.psycom.net/foods-that-help-with-anxiety-and-stress/?scrlybrkr=ab5a775a

2. Diet and Depression, *WebMD*, https://www.webmd.com/depression/guide/diet-recovery

41

AWAKENING YOUR
INNATE INTELLIGENCE

The Masgutova method, or Masgutova neurosensorimotor reflex integration (MNRI), is a specific therapy for addressing healing at a foundational neurological level. I learned about this from a colleague and sought services for my son. After seeing the benefits, I began taking classes to learn more so I could work with him more effectively and perhaps help my clients as well.

I have been practicing as an OT using the Masgutova method for over seven years, and I continue to take courses. There are helpful protocols to release stress hormones in the body that are stored when traumas occur, and for post-traumatic stress disorder (PTSD) for people of all ages. This treatment method is beneficial across the life span and is worth considering to support your health and healing.

Another reason I believe this method is effective is that the nervous system is accessed through touch. As a collective society, we are touch-deprived. Touch is crucial to overall development and provides a sense of security and comfort.

For more information about the Masgutova method, to find a practitioner near you, or to learn about training opportunities, please visit https://www.masgutovamethod.com.

42

✤⌁✤

COGNITIVE BEHAVIORAL
THERAPY (CBT)

Cognitive behavioral therapy (CBT) is a form of evidenced-based psychological treatment that has been demonstrated to be effective for a range of issues. CBT is based on several core principles:

1. Psychological issues are partly based on faulty or unhelpful ways of thinking.

2. Psychological issues are partly based on learned patterns of unhelpful behavior.

3. People suffering from psychological issues can improve by learning better ways of coping with and managing them, and this will help alleviate their symptoms.

CBT is largely based on the idea that your thoughts, emotions, and actions are connected and affect each other. In other words, the way you think and feel about something can affect what you do. CBT treatment typically involves efforts to change thinking patterns.

Over the years, I have found CBT to be helpful, and like anything, some practitioners are better than others. I appreciate a practitioner who gives me specific strategies to apply and holds me accountable to practicing to improve my mental health. I like that CBT addresses what is currently going on and doesn't focus on delving into the past so much that it takes several sessions to be given effective strategies.

In my experience, putting a label on my specific ways of thinking (cognitive distortions) and being given specific strategies for those negative thinking patterns has been very helpful. A CBT practitioner will guide you in identifying any negative thinking patterns you might have and will work with you to identify and put positive thinking strategies in place.

Source

1. Greenberger, D., & Padesky, C. A. (2016). *Mind over mood: Change how you feel by changing the way you think* (2nd ed.). Guilford Press.

2. "What is Cognitive Behavioral Therapy, " *Healthline*, https://www.healthline.com/health/cognitive-behavioral-therapy

3. "What is Cognitive Behavioral Therapy," *APA*, https://www/apa.org/ptsd-guideline/patients-and-families/cognitive-behavioral

43

✤⟡✤

UNTRADITIONAL THERAPY

I have a good friend who runs a treatment program for severe anxiety and depression through a local psychiatric group. As we became better friends and she learned about my battle with anxiety and depression, I gained the courage to ask details about the programs she ran. One was called ketamine therapy.

Ketamine can be administered through an IV or as a nasal mist. It acts within a few hours, unlike traditional antidepressants that need three to six weeks to build up in the system before therapeutic effects are noticeable. There are some factors that need to be met to qualify for ketamine treatment. It will only be considered after many other treatments have been tried and have not been effective.

The other treatment program my friend coordinated was TMS. Transcranial magnetic stimulation (TMS) is a noninvasive procedure that uses magnetic fields to stimulate nerve cells in the brain to improve symptoms of depression. TMS is typically used when other depression treatments haven't been effective. This treatment for depression involves delivering repetitive magnetic pulses to the motor cortex area of the brain. An electromagnetic coil is placed against your scalp, near the forehead. The electromagnet painlessly delivers magnetic pulses that stimulate nerve cells in the region of your brain involved in mood control and depression. This activates regions of the brain that have decreased activity in depression.

As I learned more about TMS, I felt like I met the criteria. After I met with the psychiatrist and was approved, I began treatment. TMS treatment occurred daily for many weeks. It was an opportunity for me to address the fact that I have chronic and severe depression. It was humbling. My friend came in periodically to check on me, which was also humbling. I faced my internal demons about being judged and not being good enough, but they didn't win this time. I was accepted for who I was, and my friend was helping me because she cared about me and didn't judge me. It took over a month for me to notice the effects of the TMS treatments. In my case, I didn't notice anything earth-shattering. It was subtle, but even to this day, my typical internal mood is at a higher functioning level than before. There are cases where patients go in to do more sessions to reactivate the effects. I have considered that, but haven't felt the need up to this point.

In past decades, electroconvulsive therapy (ECT), also known as shock therapy, is what people turned to when their medications and other therapies didn't help. This treatment is still available, but I didn't look into it due to the intensive nature and side effects, and because I don't believe my depression is severe enough to warrant this treatment.

Source

1. Collins, S. (2015). *What You Need to Know About Ketamine's Effects*. WebMD. ttps://www.webmd.com/depression/features/what-does-ketamine-do-your-brain

2. "Ketamine Infusion Therapy," *American Psychiatric Nurses Association*, https://www.apna.org/m/pages-therapy.cfm?pageid=6603

3. "What You Need to Know About Ketamine's Effects," *WebMD*, https://www.webmd.com/depression/features/what-does-ketamine-do-your-brain

44

✤◇✤

AFFIRMATIONS

When I think of affirmations, I immediately think of a *Saturday Night Live* skit from when I was younger, which was mocking someone who was affirming themselves. If I'm being honest, I still find affirmations uncomfortable at times, but I have learned to push through that because they are crucial to shifting toward positive self-perception and healing.

Affirmations are specific, intentional, positive statements that aim to challenge previously held negative thinking patterns and turn them into positive ones. They have the ability to influence and alter your mood, thoughts, feelings, and habits. When repeated frequently, affirmations access the subconscious mind and allow new beliefs to be established. The more frequently affirmations are repeated, the more the positive beliefs will be anchored.

It is important to use affirmations when you are in a state where you are calm and open to new ideas. In order for the affirmations to take root, you need to believe them or be open to believing them at some level.

You can find recordings of affirmations or create your own. When writing affirmations, it is important to focus on what you want to achieve. Some of my favorite affirmations are listed below:

- "I love who I am, and I am openly attracting positive relationships into my life."

- "I accept and love myself, and I accept others as they are."

- "I am focused on breathing deeply in stressful situations."

- "I am focused on achieving calm by breathing deeply throughout the day."

One thing to be aware of is that when someone with a negative self-image or low self-esteem uses affirmations, they can feel that the positive statements are in deep conflict with their prior or current negative belief system. This has been true for me. I believe this is why affirmations were initially so uncomfortable for me. I didn't believe that anything about them was true, and I wasn't at a place to believe anything other than the negative scripts I had been internalizing for years.

If you are new to affirmations and/or don't have a healthy level of self-esteem, it will be most beneficial to start with more neutral affirmations and work up to positive ones. If you start with affirmations that don't resonate at all, your brain will trigger the negative script you can more readily identify with. Neutral affirmations will most likely go under the radar and will begin to replace the negative dialogue. Some examples of neutral affirmations are listed below:

- "I am getting more confident each day."

- "I am committed to healing one day at a time."

- "I'm working on accepting myself just as I am."

- "I can feel scared and still take positive steps."

- "Just for today, I will not judge myself."

- "I'm doing my best today, and that is good enough."

- "I will not give up."

Source

1. Loethen, K. (2020, July 10). *The Power of Neutral Affirmations*. Urban Balance.

2. Reiter, D. (2007). *Dancing with Divinity - Positive Affirmations for Any Situation*.

3. "Affirmations," *Clinical Hypnotherapy*,

   https://www.clinicalhypnotherapy-cardiff.co.uk/affirmations/
4. "The Power of Neutral Affirmations," *Urban Balance,*

   https://www.urbanbalance.com/the-power-of-neutral-affirmations/

45

✤⬦✤

DISCOVER YOUR NATURE

I am drawn to personality tests. I find the interpretations interesting and helpful as I navigate the world. Over the years, these different tests have been fun and have affirmed my positive personality traits. They've also helped me to identify those traits that I need to be aware of so I can grow. The most helpful free online test I have taken in recent years is the empath test.

The first time I heard the word "empath" was a few years ago, and it immediately caught my attention. I now believe that was because I am an empath. I have often struggled with my sensitivity and how it often overtakes me in many ways. Learning more about what an empath is has really helped me.

An empath is someone who is highly attuned to the energy and emotions around them. They have the ability to sense the feelings, thoughts, and energies of living things, places, and objects. An empath is predisposed to absorb the energy around them, and this can be overwhelming if proper boundaries have not been established. Empaths often have the ability to put themselves in someone else's shoes and connect with that person and situation on a deep level. The term "empath" is derived from the word "empathy," which is the ability to understand and share the emotions of another person. An empath has a natural ability to go beyond the boundaries of empathy where others' energies and situations can negatively affect them. It is common for empaths to become stressed or sick if they take on too many negative emotions.

The term "empath" sounded an alarm in my mind. This is me. This explains why it is gut-wrenching for me to watch the news and why I can't shake a sad or disturbing story for days, weeks, or longer. If there is a situation I want to—but cannot—change or improve, it often distresses me, especially if it involves children. Being an empath explains why I feel the words of a song so deeply that it can bring me to tears. My natural sensitivity and caring for others is summed up well with this one word, and it made me feel like I wasn't alone. Being an empath has served me well in my personal and professional life. The characteristics of an empath are what drew me to my field of occupational therapy and my love of children. It has also posed challenges when I don't know what to do with the feelings I have or how to process a specific situation.

There are four sub-personality types of empaths: healer, counselor, champion, and teacher. There are many characteristics of an empath. Some of the characteristics include, but are not limited to:

Common Characteristics of an Empath

Empathetic	Deeply caring	Strong intuition	Highly sensitive
Has boundary issues	Easily overwhelmed	Problem-solver	Dislikes conflict
Holds unique views	Has difficulty fitting in	Tends to isolate oneself	Needs to recharge
Loves nature	Helper	Overwhelmed by crowds	Feels emotions of others
Compassionate	Sympathetic	Creative and imaginative	Open-minded
Warm	Independent	Tolerant	Progressive

A person's temperament is paramount in how they perceive information and how they react in all situations. Although a person is born with an innate temperament, temperament can be influenced by one's culture, upbringing, and experiences. Differences in temperament influence the way we regulate our emotions and behaviors. Through longitudinal research, Thomas and Chess (1996) developed a model of three general types of temperament: easygoing, difficult, and slow to warm.

Someone with an easygoing temperament is generally happy and active from birth and adjusts easily to new situations and environments. They have regular bodily functions, approach new situations with positivity, are highly adaptable to change, have a positive mood, and have a mild intensity of reactions to situations.

Someone with a difficult temperament typically has irregular bodily functions, tends to have negative reactions to new situations, resists and/or doesn't handle change well, is highly sensitive, and has a pessimistic view of the world. A person with a difficult temperament feels things strongly and has intense reactions to both positive and negative situations.

Someone with a slow to warm temperament is cautious. They are observant and calm. They take their time to adapt and are often inclined to withdraw from new situations. They characteristically have a low activity level and are considered to be shy.

Learning that one's temperament is developed in utero has given me a deeper understanding of my perspective and personality. I have been told many times throughout my life that I'm too sensitive and I need to grow a thicker skin. I had interpreted these types of comments as feedback that I was deficient and needed to change and adjust to situations differently. Expressing negative opinions about one's character to a sensitive person is detrimental because they internalize that negativity and add it to the layers of their "I'm not good enough" narrative. For some, taking constructive criticism is natural, but for others, depending on their temperament, it is a skill that needs to be learned. This is true for all situations and reactions. Knowing your own (and other people's) temperament is a roadmap to more positive relationships and to self-acceptance and love.

Learning the nuances and characteristics of my temperament and personality over the past several years has given me invaluable insight into who I am. It has also highlighted the importance of accepting others for who they are and where they are in their journey.

There are many free online personality and temperament tests. I encourage you to explore and take the ones that call to you. I have listed some below to get you started:

- https://psychologia.co/empathy-test/

- https://www.truity.com/test/enneagram-personality-test

- https://my-personality-test.com/true-colours

- https://www.colorquiz.com/

- https://www.focusonthefamily.com/marriage/4-animals-personality-test/

- https://www.attitude.org.nz/personality-test

- https://openpsychometrics.org/tests/O4TS/

- https://www.truity.com/test/typefinder-temperament-test

- https://centerforparentingeducation.org/library-of-articles/child-development/broad-categories/

Source

1. Chess, S., & Thomas, A. (1996). *Temperament: Theory and practice.* Brunner/Mazel.

46

❖◇❖

ADDITIONAL STRATEGIES FOR HEALTH AND WELL-BEING

Visualization

Writing down your hopes and seeing them each morning and throughout the day projects what you want to the universe. The energy and mindset you project comes back to you. Writing down your goals and hopes helps to manifest their reality. I encourage you to make a vision board. It can be as simple or as intricate and complex as you'd like. I make my vision board during the last week of the year for the following year. I usually use colored pencils and markers to draw a design and write key words and phrases. I have also seen collage-style vision boards with pictures that had been cut out of magazines. Once you have made your board, put it in a place where you will see it every day, preferably many times a day. Since I do a yearly board, I enjoy looking at it to see what I've incorporated and achieved that I had listed on my board. I incorporate the items that I still want to work on or that haven't come to fruition into my next board.

Get Moving

Exercise is important for our physical and emotional health. We were made to move. Find a workout, class, or exercise you enjoy. The most important part is committing and showing up. That is more than half of the battle.

Write It Down

It is important to express your feelings, and journaling can be very beneficial toward this end. In addition to expressing your thoughts and ideas, by journaling, you can reflect later on what you have written. It has been helpful to me to go back and reread past journal entries to understand my journey and my growth in particular areas.

Connect with Nature

There is something grounding and calming about being outside. Being outside can be centering, and when you are able to focus on something beautiful in nature, the peace inside abounds all the more. Whether it is hiking in the mountains, sitting on a patio or porch, taking a walk around the neighborhood, sitting on the beach, or walking in the forest, connecting with nature and focusing on the sights and sounds can be calming.

Meditating outside or with nature sounds can be a healing practice. There is evidence that listening to ocean sounds is calming and restorative.

Healing with Sound and Music

Music is powerful. A song can bring a flood of memories in a few notes. Music can also be prayer. I discovered Christian rock music stations over a decade ago, and they have added another element and a new depth to my prayer. For many years, I chose to listen solely to Christian rock in the car, or I'd drive in silence. I was recently reminded that any music, if it resonates with you, is good for the soul. I discovered country music in college, and I've liked it ever since. On a recent road trip, I indulged in country music the entire time and I was reminded of how happy it makes my soul. It has a much different effect on the rest of my family, but that's OK.

There are different songs and genres for different times and moods. I have listed some favorites below for specific purposes and occasions:

Songs for Reflection

- "Just Be Held" by Casting Crowns

- "I Love Me" by Demi Lovato

- "Forgiveness" by Matthew West

- "Remind Me Who I Am" by Jason Gray

- Rascal Flatts

    o "Changed"

    o "My Wish"

- "Fear Is a Liar" by Zach Williams

- "Black Train" by Josh Turner

- "Angel" by Sarah McLachlan

- "You Are More" by Tenth Avenue North

- "Humble and Kind" by Tim McGraw

- "Stand in the Light" by Jordan Smith

- "Hold On" by Michael Bublé

- "Broken and Beautiful" by Kelly Clarkson

- "Never Break Heart" by Eric Church

Songs for Praise

- "Holy Spirit" by Francesca Battistelli

- Zach Williams

  o "Chain Breaker"

  o "There Was Jesus," featuring Dolly Parton

- "Better Is One Day" by Kutless

- "God Is on the Move" by 7eventh Time Down

- "Every Good Thing" by The Afters

- "Say Amen" by Finding Favour

- "Counting Every Blessing" by Rend Collective

- "All the People Said Amen" by Matt Maher

- "Let It Rain" by Crowder and Mandisa

- "Trust in You" by Lauren Daigle

- "Blessed Be Your Name" by Matt Redman

- "God of All My Days" by Casting Crowns

Songs to Inspire and Uplift

- MercyMe

  o "Shake"

  o "Grace Got You"

  o "Greater"

- "Daisies" by Katy Perry

- "Hello, My Name Is" by Matthew West

- "Same Boat" by Zac Brown Band

- "Stronger" by Kelly Clarkson

- Mandisa

  o "Stronger"

  o "Overcomer"

- "Soul on Fire" by Third Day/All Sons & Daughters

- "Move" by Toby Mac

- Garth Brooks

  o "The River"

  o "Standing outside the Fire"

- "Live Like That" by the Sidewalk Prophets

- "Lift Your Head, Weary Sinner" by Crowder

- "If That Ain't God" by Chris Young

- "Fighter" by Christina Aguilera

- "Do Everything" by Steven Curtis Chapman

- "Higher" by Creed

- "The Mountain" by Three Days Grace

- "Start a Fire" by Unspoken

- "Brave" by Sara Bareilles

- "Here for a Reason" by Ashes Remain

- "You Are Loved" by Josh Groban

- "Stand" by Rascal Flatts

- "Fight Song" by Rachel Platten

- "Christ in Me" by Jeremy Camp

- "Survivor" by Zach Williams

- "Learning to Be the Light" by Newworldson

- "Do Life Big" by Jamie Grace

Sounds and vibrations are very powerful and can be healing. There are many therapies involving sounds and music. These include, but are not limited to, Tibetan singing bowls, sound healing, tuning forks, gong baths, om chanting, health rhythms, and sound baths.

Service

> God keeps on loving the world. He keeps on sending you and me to prove that He loves the world, that He still has that compassion for the world. It is we who have to be His love, His compassion in the world of today. But to be able to love we must have faith, for faith in action is love, and love in action is service.
> —Mother Teresa

We are called to love and help our neighbors. This can be in our own homes, down the street, and in the larger community and world. Taking the focus off myself and helping others connects me to a higher purpose and always makes me feel good and grateful.

Massage or Reflexology

We store trauma and stress in our bodies, and having physical work done can be extremely helpful. There are different types of massages to meet your needs. Physical touch is healing, and massages can be very relaxing. I have been using massage as part of my self-care regimen for years.

Creative Outlet

I have found that tapping into my creative side can be therapeutic and very rewarding. It could be taking an art class or dabbling in an area of interest on your own. Creating something that you've conceptualized and then manifested into existence is a beautiful form of self-expression. Last summer I took a ceramics class that I had been wanting to take for ten years. I had hesitated because when I took it in college, I wasn't very skilled. I'm glad that I took the class, and although I'm still not particularly skilled in ceramics, the experience was fun and fulfilling. If there is something you've been wanting to do or try, whether it's art or something else, take the plunge and explore what this new experience brings you.

I used to think being artistic and creative were the same thing. I have found many ways to express my creativity despite my non-artistic limitations. It is important to find avenues to express your creativity. My current favorite ways to express my creativity are through writing, acrylic pouring, and developing sequences for exercise classes that I teach.

47

☙❖❧

FORGIVENESS

Forgiveness is difficult. It has taken much prayer, reading, and growth to acknowledge that forgiving others and myself is crucial for healing and for true joy. Forgiving myself has proven to be much more difficult for me than forgiving others. To forgive yourself, you have to spend enough time in quiet prayer and reflection to go into the depths of your heart. Within the depths of your heart, you will slowly discover core wounds that have formed your perceptions. These perceptions lead to the tendencies of behavior and contribute to how you react in a variety of circumstances. Accepting yourself and loving yourself without judgment is key to forgiving past mistakes. Many of the wounds I had held on to for so long were decisions or situations I would have quickly forgiven others for and encouraged them to give themselves grace if they had made the same choices. Holding myself to higher standards and refusing to love the broken parts of me was extremely detrimental.

Confession has been instrumental in my ability to forgive myself and others. The realization that God wants to pour His mercy and grace upon all who sincerely seek Him and His forgiveness is overwhelming. If God, in all of His glory and majesty, desires to forgive and demands that we in turn forgive others, who am I to question that? It is extremely humbling that the Creator of the universe is willing to forgive my sins so that I can live in union with Him and work toward becoming the person He created me to be.

Initially, going to confession was extremely difficult for me. I was worried about being judged by the priest, and I was ashamed of my sins. My pride often got in my way of going, as I often tried to justify that my sins weren't that bad compared to those of others. Well, that's not how it works. We are called to be the best versions of ourselves, and that means being real with ourselves and admitting all of our wrongdoings. Admitting our sins isn't done for the sake of punishment. It is necessary to clean out the garbage to make room for God's grace and mercy in our lives.

Realizing how much God loves me has allowed me to let go of my past mistakes and sins and view them as stepping-stones to the Christ seeking woman that I am now. God loves me, and God loves you tremendously. He loves us because He created us. We are His children, and He wants to be in union with us. Sin separates us from God; therefore, it is imperative to search your soul and make amends for anything that is distancing you from a personal relationship with Him.

An examination of conscience is a tool that is used before a confession. There are many variations, but the ones I have found typically guide a person through the Ten Commandments and different ways a person could have acted against them. A friend told me about the BAKER method of examining my conscience. It was designed for daily use and is a beautiful way to end the day in prayer.

- **Blessings:** Review your day and call to mind the people, things, and events you are thankful for from the day. Draw into the attitude of gratitude and positivity.

- **Ask:** Ask the Holy Spirit for the ability to see when, where, and how you strayed from God today in your decisions, and to allow you to see your flaws and sins from today. Ask for the enlightenment to distinguish right from wrong in your heart.

- **Kill:** Acknowledge that it was sin that crucified Jesus. Let the gravity of sin penetrate your heart.

- **Embrace:** Embrace Christ and His cross and ask Him for mercy. I often envision Jesus wrapping me in His arms and embracing me. Allow Jesus's merciful love to embrace you.

- **Resolve:** Resolve to do better and not commit these sins tomorrow. It is helpful to make a concrete resolution. Start small and celebrate your success. Examples of resolutions include:

  o When tempted by a previous sin, say a "Hail Mary" or another prayer

  o Say, "Jesus, help me," any time you feel tempted

  o Do an act of kindness

  o Pray for someone that is difficult for you to get along with or that has a different viewpoint than you do

  o Read Scripture

I have to actively focus on forgiveness. I tend to let my pain overtake me if a repeat offender hurts me in some way. I must remember that holding on to that pain only hurts me and no one else. I also know that I cannot forgive on my own. I am not strong enough. I need God's help. I pray for His strength and for the grace to be able to forgive and transform my ability to love others. Realizing that I am far from perfect and that I make many mistakes increases my humility and my ability to forgive others. Attempting to see and love others as God does changes my perspective and my tendency to think that someone is being hurtful on purpose. When I take the time to give someone the benefit of the doubt and consider that there are likely many extenuating circumstances leading to a person's behavior, I tend to take it less personally.

We are called to live in harmony with others. Learning to forgive and let go of past hurts releases negative emotions and makes room for increased positivity, peace, and joy. It transforms the tendency to react out of hurt and anger into an acceptance that life is messy, people make mistakes, and we all need grace and forgiveness.

48

⊹⤝❖⤜⊹

MERCY

Mercy ties into forgiveness. In fact, many sources define mercy as the forgiveness of others. It is the decision to put aside hatred and the desire for vengeance. It is a choice to be made, regardless of the actions of another. The choice to be merciful and forgive does not nullify a person's actions or erase the damage they've done. It is a life-giving decision that allows healing to occur instead of allowing the cycle of violence and evil to continue. When I think of mercy, I also think of loving someone else the way I'd like to be treated and loved, even (or especially) when it doesn't appear that they are deserving. This is a high calling and one that is impossible without tapping into the power and strength of God and the Holy Spirit. I think of Saint Mother Teresa ministering to the poor in Calcutta. I think of serving the poor or needy in any capacity, whether it be volunteering at a food kitchen, providing reduced or free medical care, or stopping and not only giving someone money or something to eat but looking them in the eyes and letting them know that they are seen. To me, mercy is peeling back all of our layers and letting the beauty of the Holy Spirit, the crux of Jesus's mission on earth, pour out of us to let the marginalized of our society know that they are seen and loved. It is stepping out of our comfort zones and habits to notice and realize that we are called to help all of our brothers and sisters, without judgment and only love.

Before we can be merciful to others, we need to weed out anything within us that stands in the way of self-love and being merciful to ourselves. When you find something within yourself or within someone else that is blocking you from moving forward in a positive direction, stop and reflect on the reason why. What is keeping you from letting go of the hurt that remains inside of you or that is brought up by another's actions? Invite Jesus into this and ask for Him to enter and handle the situation. Ask Him to reveal the root issue (or issues) that is preventing your ability to be merciful to yourself or others.

In humility, we need to deeply feel God's love for us and realize that everything we have is a gift from Him, which we are called to share with others. First and foremost, we need to share His love. If we are to truly love as Jesus does, we need to heal our wounds and walk toward showing others mercy. It is very easy to blame others in the course of a day without considering their perspectives or intents. When we invite God into the situation, we are reminded that we, too, are broken, and we don't have the capacity to know what the other person is going through. Choose forgiveness. Choose kindness. Choose mercy.

A form of mercy that I have struggled with most is self-compassion. I have held myself to a higher standard in many ways, and forgiveness hasn't come easily for me. I have often judged myself unfairly and internalized shame when I haven't measured up to unrealistic expectations. I am learning to accept the younger versions of myself and nurture who I was then and who I am now. Dr. Kristin Neff has done groundbreaking research on self-compassion and has created many books, videos, and other resources to help on the journey of self-compassion.

49

✦━◇━✦

OPTIMIZE YOUR BRAIN

I am open to the possibility of healing in alternative ways. I believe that there is a place for both traditional and holistic/alternative medicine and therapies. Technology has its pros and cons, but the therapy I talk about in this chapter is an example of the benefits of blending research, science, and technology.

I have learned that it is important to go beyond the symptoms that may manifest in the body and address the root cause of disease. Stress, injury, and traumatic events can interrupt the brain's natural abilities to process information, communicate, and complete tasks efficiently. Energy flows through both hemispheres of the brain, and each hemisphere has specific functions. When energy gets stuck in one or both hemispheres, imbalance occurs and can result in a myriad of dysfunction.

The left hemisphere of the brain is responsible for the parasympathetic division of the autonomic nervous system (ANS). If the left hemisphere is dominant, then depressive energy manifests due to a freeze or brake indicator to the system.

The sympathetic nervous system is housed in the right hemisphere of the brain. When activated, the sympathetic nervous system produces the fight or flight response. If there is an imbalance of energy and the right hemisphere is dominant, the system is most likely in a constant state of fight or flight. This could manifest as panicking, not being able to turn thoughts off, or being hypervigilant or constantly on guard even when you are physically safe. The brain is sending messages to flee or to escape a potential threat of danger.

I learned about Cereset from a coworker who is like-minded and found great benefit from this therapy. Cereset is a noninvasive technology that enables your brain to relax, rebalance, and reset itself so you can regain your ability to function at your highest level and feel better. Much like the Masgutova method (MNRI), Cereset is founded on the principle that the brain is capable of healing itself. This program uses technology to relax the brain and rebalance and unfreeze areas where energy is stuck.

Cereset uses the patented Brain Echo technology that empowers the brain to reset itself as it hears brain-initiated sounds and uses reflection and resonance of brainwave rhythms to balance the brain naturally.

When the brain is balanced the result is often better sleep, release of chronic stress, the ability to cope and manage emotions and situations with increased peace and calm, and better ability to focus and comprehend.

Source

1. "How Can Cereset Help You," *Cereset,* https://www.cereset.com

50

⊹◈⊹

THE FIX

You can't go back and change the beginning, but you
can start where you are and change the ending.
—C. S. Lewis

As you might have deduced from the number of strategies I have
tried along my journey, I was looking for a fix. I wanted a cure,
and I didn't want to have to deal with anxiety and depression or the
shame that came with them. I have realized that there isn't a quick fix,
and the times when I have accepted my crosses are often the times when
I've felt the most grace from God and the truest to myself. I was afraid
of suffering and was seeking to only feel good. That is not life. There are
wonderful moments and much goodness in life, and I have learned to be
more present so I can fully enjoy them. What I continue to work on is
not seeking good to replace or displace the uncomfortable or hurt I am
feeling. I have learned to sit and be still. In the quiet moments, I have
gained a true understanding of myself and of what is important. I have
learned that suffering isn't a bad thing, and when we offer it as a sacrifice
to God, it can bring healing to ourselves and to many others. Jesus died
on the cross for me. He died on the cross for you. His suffering is the
ultimate of all sufferings. He knows our pain because He has felt it.
Ask Him to come into your suffering and pain. Consider joining your
suffering to Him and offering it for a loved one or for a cause close to

your heart. The circumstances may not change, but the knowledge that God wants to work all things for your good will slowly be revealed. God didn't promise a life without suffering. He promised to be there amid the suffering, and He is there and He will always show up. I encourage you to take the first step and invite Him into your suffering, your joys, and your entire journey. Let God guide you. Let Him lead you toward the next step in your life. Let Him be with you in the silence and the chaos. He wants you to open your heart to Him. Wherever you are in your journey, do not give up. God's mercy and forgiveness are endless. There is nothing you have done that will or can prevent Him from loving you. His love is too great. God's love is immense beyond our comprehension. You are loved.

I am a work in progress, as I believe we all are, if we are honest with ourselves. Please know that, by writing this book, I am in no way stating that I am struggle-free and don't have difficult days. Rather, I have realized that there are many factors, therapies, and strategies that I have tried and that have been helpful in one way or another. I am providing these resources which I have encountered on my journey thus far to hopefully provide an easier way of discovering options to put positive paving stones on your path instead of having to unturn many heavy boulders.

Although I have spent a lot of time discovering and trying to heal, a factor has emerged that is invaluable. No matter the state I am in during a day, a week, a year, or during my lifetime, I am precious and beautiful just as I am—and you are, too. My inability to know this and to truly believe that God loves me unconditionally was at the root of my shame and self-loathing. Once I was able to hear that God loved me and called me to love myself, not for what I accomplished but because I existed, things started to shift.

The bottom line is that there is no fix. There is no cure-all. There can be enlightenment, healing, self-discovery, and immense growth. Regardless of any strategy or therapy you try, without God, there won't be long-term healing. Healing is a process, and God wants you to invite Him into your journey. Give yourself grace, especially on those hard days. Most importantly, know that you are never alone. Never.

51

~✦~

HONOR YOURSELF

One of my main purposes for writing this book has been to provide ideas and resources that you may not have encountered and that can help you. Through the process of writing this book, and through continued self-awareness, acceptance, and development, a theme has arisen: honor yourself. On our journeys we encounter helpful people, resources, and practices. More importantly, as we journey, it is imperative that we encounter and take time to uncover our true selves. It can be a long and laborious process, but as you uncover your truth and your beauty, regardless of what society and other judgmental resources say, honor yourself. God has equipped you with an intuition to know what is right for you in all circumstances. This intuition is the "gut feeling" or the "little voice" that guides you periodically. If you take time to harness it and listen to it, this feeling and/or voice will become louder and easier to follow. Take the time to connect with God or your spirituality to awaken the ability to acknowledge and follow the nudging of the Holy Spirit and the universe. We were created to seek God and a higher purpose than ourselves. Our purpose is to lose ourselves (our pride, arrogance, self-reliance, and selfishness), and increase our humility and docility to God so that we can become the women and men He intended us to be.

Throughout my life I had used society and others as points of reference to determine what I should do and what is OK and what isn't.

This was exhausting and extremely detrimental. I was using inaccurate gauges to judge myself. It took me decades to realize that I am enough just as I am. I am enough because God loves me and willed me into being. I don't need to prove anything to anyone, and neither do you. You are enough, and you are loved.

Accepting myself and forgiving myself continues to be part of my journey, and it can be difficult. I am now working on validating myself and my choices against my virtues and morals, not against the world's standards. In our country, this is very counterintuitive and far from popular. I am learning and working on being at peace when someone doesn't value my choices or viewpoints. This is challenging for this people-pleaser, but I am shifting each day to honor myself from the vantage point of how God sees me and what His will is for me. I know that God wants all of His children to love themselves for who they are and to completely depend on Him for everything. Realizing that God loves you now, just as you are, with all of your flaws and past mistakes, is humbling and healing. It is a game changer to let this unconditional love and acceptance settle into your bones and soul. It will change the way you operate in your life and how you perceive things. It most likely won't be a huge aha moment, but gradually, things will shift. I am continuing to let the concept that God truly loves me, all of me, resonate so that I completely embrace it. Accepting that God loves me has helped me accept and love myself. Invite God into your life. No matter your circumstances. No matter your mistakes. No matter how far gone you might feel things are. It is never too late. God is waiting to embrace you and guide you toward the best version of yourself.

Maia is available for speaking events and workshops in which she infuses a variety of the strategies shared in this book. If your organization is interested, please inquire at faithfilledwellness.org

REFERENCES

Adverse Childhood Experiences (ACEs). (n.d.). Retrieved July 3, 2021, from https://www.cdc.gov/violenceprevention/aces/index.html

American Psychiatric Nurses Association. (2016). *Ketamine Infusion Therapy*. American Psychiatric Nurses Association.

Beaulieu, J. (2010). *Human Tuning Sound Healing with Tuning Forks*. Lightning Source Incorporated.

Brown, Brené. 2004. *Women and Shame: Reaching Out, Speaking Truths, and Building Connection*. 3C Press.

Brown, Brené. 2007. *I Thought It Was Just Me (but it isn't): Making the Journey from "What Will People Think?" to "I Am Enough"*. Avery.

Brown, Brené. 2010. *The Gifts of Imperfection: Let Go of Who You Think You're Supposed to Be and Embrace Who You Are*. Hazelden Publishing.

Brown, Brené. 2013. *How the Courage to Be Vulnerable Transforms the Way We Live, Love, Parent, and Lead*. Avery.

Brown, Brené. 2017. *Rising Strong: How the Ability to Reset Transforms the Way We Live, Love, Parent, and Lead*. Random House.

Burton, M. (2019). *Exercise and Depression*. Independently Published.

Campbell, C. C. (2012). *My Sisters the Saints*. Image.

Catholic Online-St. Dymphna-Saints & Angels. (n.d.). Catholic Online. https://www.catholic.org/saints/saint.php?saint_id=222

Challem, J. (2007). *The food-mood solution.* Wiley.

Collins, S. (2015). *What You Need to Know About Ketamine's Effects.* WebMD. ttps://www.webmd.com/depression/features/what-does-ketamine-do-your-brain

Dale, C. (2015). *Llewellyn's Complete Book of Chakras: Your Definitive Source of Energy Center Knowledge for Health, Happiness, and Spiritual Evolution (Llewellyn's Complete Book Series 7).* Llewellyn Worldwide.

Danylchuk, L. (2019). *Yoga Practices for Trauma Recovery.* Routledge.

Diet And Depression. (n.d.). WebMD. https://www.webmd.com/depression/guide/diet-recovery

DSouza, R. J. (2019, August 29). *Affirmations | Benefits Of Affirmations | Create Affirmations.* https://www.clinicalhypnotherapy-cardiff.co.uk/affirmations/

Dyer, J. (2017). *Empath: A Complete Guide for Developing Your Gift and Finding Your Sense of Self.* Pristine Publishing.

Dyer, J. (2018). *The Highly Sensitive: How to Stop Emotional Overload, Relieve Anxiety, and Eliminate Negative Energy.* CreateSpace Independent Publishing Platform.

Emerson, D., Hopper, E., Cope, S., Van der Kolk, B., & Levine, P. A. (2011). *Overcoming Trauma through Yoga: Reclaiming Your Body.* North Atlantic Books.

Faber, S. (2020, May 5). *The Toxic Twelve Chemicals and Contaminants In Cosmetics.* Environmental Working Group. https://www.ewg.org/the-toxic-twelve-chemicals-and-contaminants-in-cosmetics

Felitti, Vincent, "et al. ", 1998. "The Adverse Childhood Experiences (ACE) Study: Leading Determinants of Health." Volume 4, Issue 4: p245-258.

Fight the New Drug. https://fightthenewdrug.org/

Fondin, M. S. (2018). *Chakra healing for vibrant energy.* New World Library.

Gaynor, M. L. (2002). *The Healing Power of Sound.* Shambhala Publications.

Goldman, J. (2015). *Sound Healing for Beginners.* Llewellyn Worldwide.

Greenberger, D. (2015). *Mind Over Mood, Second Edition.* Guilford Publications.

Harris, N. B. (2018). *Deepest Well.* Houghton Mifflin Harcourt.

Hollis, R. (2018). *Girl, Wash your Face.* Thomas Nelson.

Hollis, R. (2019). *Girl, Stop Apologizing.* HarperCollins Leadership.

Kaplan, B. J. (2021). *Better Brain.* Houghton Mifflin Harcourt.

Kelly, Matthew. (2017). *Perfectly Yourself.* Blue Sparrow.

Leeds, J. (2010). *The power of sound.* Healing Arts Press.

Loethen, K. (2020). *The Power Of Neutral Affirmations.* Urban Balance. https://www.urbanbalance.com/the-power-of-neutral-affirmations/

McCarthy, J. (2018). *Harmful Ingredients Found In Candles.* Joyous Health. https://www.joyoushealth.com/27279-blog-harmful-ingredients-found-in-candles

McKusick, E. D. (2014). *Tuning the human biofield*. Healing Arts Press.

M.D., J. O. (2015). *The Power of Surrender*. Harmony.

Miller, A. (2018). *The Anti-Anxiety Diet*. Simon and Schuster.

Mueller, M. K. (2010). *8 to Great: The Powerful Process for Positive Change*. Insight, inc.

Neff, Kristin, PH. D (2011) *Self-Compassion*. William Morroe.

Orloff, J. (2010). *Emotional Freedom*. Harmony.

Orloff, J. (2012). *Dr. Judith Orloff's Guide to Intuitive Healing*. Harmony.

Orloff, J. (2017). *The Empath's Survival Guide*. Sounds True.

Orloff, J. (2019). *Thriving as an Empath*. Sounds True.

Otto, M. W. (2011). *Exercise for mood and anxiety*. OUP USA.

Padesky, C. A. (2012). *Clinician's Guide to Mind Over Mood, First Edition*. Guilford Press.

Polya, A. J. (2012). *Mind Over Matter: The Power of Emotional Intelligence*. Xlibris Corporation.

Publishing, F. C. (2011). *New American Revised Bible*. Fireside Catholic Publishing.

Qualls, L. (2020). *The Connected Parent*. Harvest House Publishers.

Ramsey, D. (2021). *Eat to Beat Depression and Anxiety*. HarperCollins.

Rand, W. L. (2000). *Reiki*. Visions Publications.

Reiter, D. (2007). *Dancing with Divinity - Positive Affirmations for Any Situation.*

Robins, R. (2014). *Positive Affirmations.* CreateSpace.

S. (2020). *What Are Chakras? Meaning, Location, And How To Unblock Them.* Healthline. https://www.healthline.com/health/what-are-chakras

Scherschligt, Dr. M., & Hinkle, Dr. T. (2005). *Holy Family School Of Faith.* Holy Family School Of Faith. https://www.schooloffaith.com/

Schuchts, Bob (2014). *Be Healed: A Guide to Encountering the Powerful Love of Jesus in Your Life.* Ave Maria Press.

Shapiro, F. (n.d.). *What Is EMDR?* EMDR Institute - Eye Movement Desensitization and Reprocessing Therapy. Retrieved July 4, 2021, from https://www.emdr.com/what-is-emdr/

Shields, B. (2005). *Down Came the Rain.* Hachette UK.

Stapely, L. (2014). *The Power of Affirmations - 1,000 Positive Affirmations.* CreateSpace.

Svetlana Masgutova Educational Institute. (n.d.). Retrieved July 3, 2021, from http://www.Masgutovamethod.com

Tang, A., Crawford, H., Morales, S., Degnan, K. A., Pine, D. S., & Fox, N. A. (2020). *Infant behavioral inhibition predicts personality and social outcomes three decades later.* Proceedings of the National Academy of Sciences.

Truschel, J. (2019, October 9). *Beat Anxiety: 8 Foods That Help With Anxiety And Stress.* Psycom.Net. https://www.psycom.net/foods-that-help-with-anxiety-and-stress/?scrlybrkr=ab5a775a

Van Der Kolk, B. A. (2014). *The Body Keeps the Score: Brain, Mind, and Body in the Healing of Trauma.* (7th ed.). Viking.

Van Nuys, David. 2015. "Brain, Mind, and Body in the Healing of Trauma." *The Neuropsychotherapist* 12: 22–31.

Vision Pursue. Retrieved October 23, 2022 from https://visionpursue. com/performance-mindset/

W., L. C. (2016). *Physical Exercise Interventions for Mental Health.* Cambridge University Press.

Wauters, A. (2002). *The Book of Chakras.* B.E.S. Publishing.

WebMD - Better Information. Better Health. WebMD. Retrieved July 3, 2021, from http://www.webmd.com

Wentz, I. (2017). *Hashimoto's Protocol.* HarperCollins.

Werner-Gray, L. (2020). *Anxiety-Free with Food.* Hay House.

Young Living Essential Oils | World Leader In Essential Oils. (n.d.). Retrieved July 3, 2021, from http://www.youngliving.com

Young, S. (2004). *Jesus Calling: Enjoying Peace in His Presence.* Integrity Publishers.

Zielinski, Eric. 2022. "13 Chemicals In Laundry Detergent & How To Avoid Them!" Natural Living Family. Accessed December 26, 2019. https://naturallivingfamily.com/chemicals-laundry-detergent-ingredients-dangers/

CPSIA information can be obtained
at www.ICGtesting.com
Printed in the USA
JSHW021103210623
43527JS00002B/13